ENDORSEMENT

I've known Michael Kuk for many years and have found him to be as knowledgeable on firefighting equipment and tactics in general as anyone I have ever known in fire service command positions. But, few of us will ever get to experience, as he did, firefighting in a war zone. In the fire service, we joke about putting the wet stuff on the red stuff as the basic principle of the job, this of course is an oversimplification, but in a war zone a whole other layer of complexity is added to the equation. Chief Kuk delves into this little known, rarely written about, aspect of firefighting. His U. S. Army tours in Viet Nam as a Firefighter Station Chief/Corporal put him in the middle of the action, all of which certainly gives him the insight and experience to write this important work. As he explains in the book, it was not only the firefighting and rescue duties with limited personnel, indiscriminate rocket attacks, constant supply shortages and various equipment malfunctions in a tropical environment, but also dealing with U. S. government bureaucracy along with the politics and unknown hazards of operating in a foreign country.

Chief Kuk has done a great service by writing this book, not only for preserving the history but also as a reference for future military firefighters in similar situations. This book is a must read for anyone interested in military firefighting.

—Frank McMenamin, D.D.S.
Former Chicago fireman
Founding member of the Fire Museum of Greater Chicago
Author of *Fight for Chicago, a Firefighter's Perspective of the Chicago Fire, October 8-9, 1871*
And *Badges of Extinction, a Synoptical History of Badges of the Paid Fire Department from 1857 to the Sesquicentennial, 2008*

Chief Michael Kuk has told the story from a party who lived it in Viet Nam during those black years. It is well that he has done this for had he not it is likely that fire and its management would, as they did in World War II, have gone unknown.

I am honored to review your book. What a book it is. It offered so much of the Viet Nam story that I did not know. Being the last living member of the 1204th Army Engineer Fire Fighting Platoon it is of great interest to me to see the changes in Military firefighting in three decades.

Yours was a world in which I would have been lost. It is fascinating story and book.

Hope it will find a place in the libraries of: The Center of Military History The Army's History Center at Carlisle's Barracks, Pennsylvania. The Curator of the COE Museum, Eric Reinert, Ft Belvoir, VA The COE Office of History, Ft. Belvoir, VA. The Engineer Center at Ft. Leonard Wood, MO. The Curator, Troy Morgan, of the Engineer Museum at Ft. Leonard Wood, MO.

From a Brother Smoke Eater, Chief, well done!

—T/5 James G. Davis U. S. Army WWII.
Member and Historian 1204th Army Engineer Fire Fighting Platoon
North Africa – Italy – France – Germany World War II
—Oldest living Army Firefighter

Firefighters around the world are a special breed of individuals. It takes a special kind of individual to assume the awesome duty and responsibility to protect others from everyday risks and hazards encountered in life. It's a difficult and challenging job, and personal "calling" reserved for an elite group of individuals. Firefighting under wartime conditions is even more challenging. Whether you are a military veteran or not, you will be instantly enthralled with the challenges and daily encounters of firefighting in a war zone as Chief Kuk takes us on a "tour of duty" as a firefighter in Vietnam in 1970-1971.

Of particular note is Chief Kuk's personal experience of how badly Vietnam Veterans were treated once they came back home. Job discrimination abounded everywhere. Returning to school, or even dating in public was not a pleasant experience for many as they tried to resume the lives they left behind when they answered their country's call to duty.

An *Army Fire Fighter in Vietnam* is a unique revelatory view of fire fighting through the eyes of those that are a special part of our Noble Breed.

—Chief (Ret.) Bill Peterson, CFIFireE, USNR ('67-'73)

"Highly recommend! Chief Kuk does an excellent job of bringing to light the experience of the "Vietnam Firefighter". I had no idea of the battles faced by our Vietnam Firefighters until I read this book. These warriors, their courage and can-do attitude are an inspiration to today's military firefighters".

—Marsh Fiedler, MSgt (retired), USAF and US Army Fire Chief

"An Army Firefighter In Vietnam" is a story of sacrifice and service of those unsung heroes who ran into danger to suppress fires in dangerous and explosive situations, quite often under unwavering fire from the enemy. Mike Kuk has captured the day to day challenges and duties of the Soldier Firefighter in a way we can all understand. This long overdue book chronicles the contributions and sacrifices of the U. S. Army's Soldier-Firefighter during the Vietnam conflict. How sad it has taken so long for America to acknowledge the sacrifices America's military men and women made in Vietnam. I remember reading of cousin David Earl Hartsoe's extraordinary heroism while serving as a Machine Gunner with Company L, Third Battalion, Ninth Marines, THIRD Marine Division (Reinforced), Fleet Marine Force, in the Republic of Vietnam on the evening of 20 May 1967. With complete disregard for his own safety, he held his own position until mortally wounded. He is interred at Gettysburg a few yards from where President Lincoln gave his famous address. I recall the fears and concerns my mother and siblings had while my 59 year old father, served in Vietnam 1968-69 and returned home via medical flight to Walter Reed hospital in Washington, DC to be medically retired from active duty. Now, some forty plus years since America's military withdrew from Vietnam, those veterans who served and survived are being recognized, a recognition so long overdue. My dear friend and colleague Mike Kuk has captured the story of the Soldier Firefighter and documented their contributions and achievements. Thanks Mike for a job well done in *An Army Firefighter In Vietnam"*

—Bill Killen, President/CEO
National Fire Heritage Center

During time of war there are many unsung heroes that in their own way contribute to the war effort. One such group of men, the Army Combat Firefighters that served in Vietnam whose stories will not be found in the many books written or movies produced about the war until now. Their heroic efforts saved many lives and saved millions of dollars in government property. Fire Chief Michael Kuk's book, "An Army Firefighter In Vietnam 1970-1971" documents the men, their fire apparatus, day to day activities and the hazards the combat firefighter endured. Chief Kuk's firsthand knowledge as a station crew chief at the Long Binh Combat Base gives the reader, be it the newest rookie firefighter to anyone interested in the fire service a great look at the war through the eyes of the Army firefighters. The book includes many photographs documenting the men and the hazards they faced. As a former military firefighter I highly recommend his book and salute him for his service to our country during the Vietnam War.

—Ted Heinbuch
Former Army Firefighter
U.S. Military Fire Apparatus Historian

AN ARMY FIREFIGHTER IN VIETNAM 1970 - 1971

FIRE CHIEF EMERITUS MICHAEL LOUIS KUK

UNITED STATES ARMY 51M

Copyright © 2023 Michael Louis Kuk.

All rights reserved. No part of this book may be reproduced, stored, or transmitted by any means—whether auditory, graphic, mechanical, or electronic—without written permission of both publisher and author, except in the case of brief excerpts used in critical articles and reviews. Unauthorized reproduction of any part of this work is illegal and is punishable by law.

ISBN: 979-8-88640-992-5 (sc)
ISBN: 979-8-88640-993-2 (hc)
ISBN: 979-8-88640-994-9 (e)

Because of the dynamic nature of the Internet, any web addresses or links contained in this book may have changed since publication and may no longer be valid. The views expressed in this work are solely those of the author and do not necessarily reflect the views of the publisher, and the publisher hereby disclaims any responsibility for them.

One Galleria Blvd., Suite 1900, Metairie, LA 70001
1-888-421-2397

INDEX

Dedication xiii
Foreword by L. Allen Ward... xv
Foreword.. xix

The Installation of Long Binh..1
General Operations...6
The Fire Stations..9
Alarms, Radios, and Dispatching..11
Fire Engines and Apparatus..15
Apparatus Exhaust and the Station's Environment 26
Fire Hose and Nozzles...28
Water Supply..30
Rescue and Medical Equipment..32
Fire Fighting Foam, AFFF, and other Extinguishing Agents............35
Haunting Health Issues from the Extinguishing Agents..................39
Mess, Food and Drink 41

The Soldier-Firefighters 44

Cuu Hoa 48

The Drug Environment... 50

Off Post Response and Security... 51

Weather and Fires 53

A Fire at the 24th EVAC.. 54

Smoke Eaters.. 56

The Burning Assignments... 58

The Agent Orange Connection 60

No SCBA and the Aftermath 62

Our Turnout Clothing 64

"Silvers" and the Asbestos Exposure 67

Badges and Identification.. 70

General Firefighting and Responses 72

Saigon Fire Brigade 74

Downed Aircraft Challenges 78

Water, Water, and Leeches.. 82

The Unsafe Practices of Live Ordnance Firefighting 84

Apparatus Positions and Response... 87

Road Hazards and Injuries on Responses 88

Eye and Vision Injuries.. 93

Dental Care or Lack There of.. 94

A Close Call in the Air 96

The Orphanage.. 98

In the Dark and Alone on a Response 100

Post 1's Pillbox 102

The Warehouse District and a Saboteur's Act 105
Medals, Recognition, and Records 110
Another Rocket – Another Fire 112
Fire Scene Investigations and Incidents... 114
Smells and Related Affairs.. 118
The Tugboat Fire and a Fatality 119
Assisting the Medics.. 121
The Port of Saigon and the Docks.. 122
The Unusual at Sea 125
A Road on Fire.. 130
Grass Fires... 134
Riots and Fires at Long Binh Jail... 137
The Dump and the Burning Pit Fires... 140
Funny Fires 142
The Negative Side of Funny Fires.. 144
A Recap of the PenePrime Fires... 147
The General Westmoreland Relationship 150
Touching Home via HAM Radio... 154
R 'n' R and an Unsuitable Ending 156
Film, Photos and Polaroids.. 158
The Firehouse Mascot 159
Holidays and Special Occasions 161
Hail & Farewell with the Vietnamese Firefighters 162
The Big Hail & Farewell with the PA&E Chief Fire Officers......... 164
Coming Home... 166
A Changed Body... 170

Return to Church 172
A Private Party and the New Music Scene 176
Dislike and Disrespect for the Vietnam Veteran 179
The Old College Try 181
The Hometown Blow 183
A Preparation for Life and Career 187
Prayers all the time 189
A Shadow of Shame 191
The VA and Me 193
Marriage, a Miscarriage, and Love on the Rocks 195
Chief Petersen's Inspiration 202
A Final Comment 204
Retrospect 206
The CD from Communications 209
Legend 211
Photo Section 215
About the Author 277

There is no doubt that I desire to dedicate this writing to all of our Country's Veterans, Patriots, and countless Unsung Heroes, who never turned their backs on America in her time of need.

They knew from their first step into service for their Country that freedom took sacrifice, courage, dedication, and a belief in God to preserve for our way of life.

And their families, friends, and loved ones, although seldom mentioned, also had to share and sacrifice the absence of their service member.

"Greater love hath no man, than to lay down one's life for another."

FOREWORD

I am delighted to write this foreword, not only because Michael Kuk has been a mentor, friend and brother firefighter for more than twenty years, but also because I believe deeply in preserving the history of the Army Combat Firefighter.

Fire Chief Emeritus Michael L. Kuk is a reliable narrator – authentic and engaging - providing readers with relevant details about his service as a combat firefighter during the Vietnam War and the years following. While Chief Kuk is an avid firefighting historian and has published numerous articles on the history of firefighting, An Army Firefighter in Vietnam, chronicles his personal journey as a combat firefighter while serving at Long Binh, the largest U.S. Army base camp in Vietnam. He is able to weave riveting accounts of his combat firefighter experience with analysis and self-examination. This book should be a required reading for anyone – civilian or soldier – who is interested in how a military firefighter thinks and feels during a war environment.

This work serves well those interested in Army firefighting history. Fire Chief Emeritus Michael L. Kuk's, An Army Firefighter in Vietnam, provides the reader with a glimpse of the daily life and the dangers inherent of a combat firefighter while serving at the largest U.S. Army military installation, Long Binh, during the Vietnam War. His stories describe not only how the firefighters operated in a war environment but also the inherent dangers.

Chief Kuk is regarded as an influential fire chief, historian of army firefighting and strong supporter of the Army combat firefighter. I am proud to call him my friend.

—L. Allen Ward, Master Sergeant (Retired)
Author of Army Firefighting, A Historical Perspective
Army Firefighter and Historian Bradenton, Florida

AN ARMY FIREFIGHTER IN VIETNAM 1970-1971

FIRE CHIEF EMERITUS MICHAEL LOUIS KUK, PHD.

FOREWORD

This writing began from the initial request of a life-long friend and retired Director U. S. Navy Fire & Emergency Services, Chief Bill Killen, who needed my help in obtaining some long lost history of Vietnam era military crash-fire-rescue trucks for a new book that he was undertaking.

Once I started researching and writing about the various military crash trucks which I worked with, I found out that revisiting my life and war experience as a young 51M military firefighter in the United States Army in Vietnam was a story worth telling on its own.

Although almost a half century has passed, my memory has come alive in revisiting my time of service. One item of historical note continued to lead to another point of interest. There were times when I could not remember all of the intricate detail, and I may have missed a point.

I did find it very disappointing that no fire department records exist from Long Binh. Even the Army's DA 5-1 Fire Reports do not exist. I assumed that everything was tracked and stored on the "Micro-Fiche" files from that era. Not so. Much has been lost now to unknown history.

One can only assume that when America pulled out of the Vietnam conflict, many things collapsed, and countless details have vaporized in the aftermath of the cloud of war.

One item that I wish I could put down in print in this writing is a detailed roster of all the soldier-firefighters names who served with me. My notes got lost through the years of travel and work location changes. Maybe one day a list can be re-discovered and everyone can be recognized.

Throughout the years of my published works and writings for fire service magazines since 1974, I made mention at several times in various fire, veteran and civilian periodicals that I hoped to re-connect to these men. Unfortunately, there have been no results.

The fire crew chief of the ammo dump detachment and I have re-established contact. He has also faced the same challenge that I have in finding any of our men. Even with today's mass media and social friendly technology, there is no easy method to locate any of our former teammates.

I do hope that this document contributes a valid source of history for the U. S. Army's Soldier-Firefighter during that conflict. So much information can be lost if someone does not write it down. Keeping part of our military's good works alive from that era is important.

What this writing might tell is how a small and very talented group of 51Ms contributed to the war effort in Vietnam during a point in our country's military history in a foreign country. The firefighters' support of our troops was remarkable, courageous, and honorable.

There were only twenty-one of us total in this assignment. We were hand-picked and assigned to USARV Special Troops. We were truly unique in how we came about, and what duties we performed while in Vietnam. The title "Combat Firefighter" is honorably ascribed.

It should be noted that every Soldier-Firefighter was a highly skilled and trained 11-Bravo (Light Weapons Infantry), who was in the upper 10% of their Advanced Individual Training (AIT).

Two Specialist-4 driver/operators came from transportation units, with excellent driving and mechanic talents, and they also were previous 11-Bravos.

Our duty and work was going to take us everywhere, thus the requirement for one to have entrusted combat skills. Once we arrived at an incident, we were pretty much on our own. Thus, self-protection and survival was paramount. We had to be ready for either firefighting or a firefight. Sometimes our assignment required both.

Plenty has been written about the Vietnam War throughout the years. A plethora of books and video documentaries are out there detailing about every aspect of the war, except the in-country American military firefighters from the various service branches.

Although our primary and expected enemy was "Old Man Fire", we did not forget that our true enemy was composed of two determined communist armies, fighting for their beliefs of the spread and sustainment of Communism worldwide.

The principal martial force was the regular and professional military army known as the North Vietnamese Army (NVA). The second threat was the Viet Cong (VC), who were actually a somewhat well unified and organized system of civilian cell fighting groups. They grew into a respected combatant version of determined and tough fighters.

The VC did not wear any manner of a true uniform, yet they were becoming a true terroristic band of enemy fighters during this timeframe. Both groups inflicted death and serious injury to our forces and our allies. And they remained vigilant to destroying our in-country installations and bases, methods and points of supply, and any war materials for the allied cause.

Despite these challenges of war and forthcoming unknowns in the performance of our duties, every U. S. Army Soldier-Firefighter stood tall and performed in an outstanding manner.

Courage was our watchword!

THE INSTALLATION OF LONG BINH

The United States Army installation of Long Binh, located approximately twenty three miles northeast of Saigon, was one of America's largest constructed military bases ever conceived to support a foreign theater of war. It was a very busy place, and its firefighters took no rest.

Long Binh Post was located on the eastern border of the Dong Nai River, and South Vietnam's Highway 1 would take one approximately twenty three miles northeast out of the city of Saigon to the installation. After the war ended, the North Vietnamese government renamed Saigon as Ho Chi Minh City.

The United States Air Force had an allied base called Bien Hoa Air Base nearby, and Long Binh's location was approximately ten miles southeast from that airfield.

The military installation served as the largest U.S Army base in Vietnam, and was home to the United States Army Vietnam (USARV) command headquarters, and its closely related Logistics Center. Troop strength reached levels of 60,000 personnel.

A few nicknames were applied to the installation during its operational period. It was called "LBJ" for two reasons. The first was because of the unofficial application of Long Binh Junction in recognition of the then-President Lyndon B. Johnson. The second had to do with its military stockade or prison. It was infamously called "Long Binh Jail".

Around 1967 the Army started realizing the serious scope of the war, and decided to resolve centralization, security, and troop billeting issues, thus moving a large collection of units to Long Binh. In unison with our allies, Long Binh became the heartbeat of the overall war effort.

Some of the major units were the II Field Force, 1st Aviation Brigade, 18th Military Police Brigade, 44th Medical Brigade, 24th and 93rd Evacuation Hospitals. The 266th Supply and Service Battalion provided graves registration, clothing and equipment, Petroleum-Oil-Lube (POL), and construction supplies for the III Corps. The 90th Replacement Battalion took in newly arrived enlisted personnel for assignment throughout the theatre of operations in South Vietnam. And of course, the military prison known as Long Binh Stockade or "Long Binh Jail".

A special note about Long Binh Jail or the prison. It was a very rough place. The detailed MP correctional soldiers had their hands full all the time. There was plenty of unrest and in-prison fighting amongst the incarcerated troops. Sometimes there were riots and set fires. LBJ was the major jail facility in Vietnam for military prisoners convicted of various crimes or waiting for trial. Some were eventually sent stateside to Fort Leavenworth, Kansas for major crimes and offences, and long term incarceration. The story about LBJ would be a book unto its own.

Long Binh did get a bloody nose from the hands of the Viet Cong on February 4, 1967. The VC conducted a successful offensive operation in destroying approximately 15,000 high explosive 155mm artillery projectiles. It was no longer considered to be a safe military facility. Our enemy was bold enough to bring their war out of the jungle to the living room of a major military installation. Security of the installation rocketed to a new high after that attack.

The major civilian contractor at Long Binh was Pacific Architects and Engineers (PA&E). As the war progressed in time, most of the post's support functions were absorbed by the PA&E contract personnel. PA&E hired US leadership and managers, then contracted with the local Vietnamese civilian labor force, who passed security background checks to come and work in a wide variety of jobs. The local Vietnamese were happy for the work and good paychecks.

The base did have some recreational facilities for the troops. Current and popular Hollywood movies were shown on any given night in several of the various troop areas. Snack bars, a craft shop, a bowling alley, a couple of nightclubs, several barber shops, and a few swimming pools were located throughout the installation. Armed Forces radio and TV were also 24/7.

Long Binh also became known as the home of the Bob Hope Show. It boasted a true outdoor amphitheater, constructed in a historically driven Roman style and fashion. Excellent sound quality and visual aspects were the result of its construction. It was huge and impressive.

Bob Hope and his entourage would perform their largest in-country Christmas show there. He would always bring other popular guest artists to entertain the troops in addition to his show. It was a special treat for all of us to see this performance, and it was quite a morale booster.

There were a couple of dental clinics, and a basketball and tennis court too. One main Post Exchange existed. Chase Manhattan Bank operated a full service branch bank, although the currency was issued in Vietnamese for in country transactions. US dollars were a true "black market" commodity within the war zone. And yes, the Black Market was alive and well.

Initial construction of Long Binh began around 1965 and the installation remained in the Army's command until 1972 when it was then turned over to the South Vietnamese Army as part of the de-escalation of the war effort. There was no family housing because the installation was located in a war zone. It grew into a true military city, and was considered a good duty station.

Today the overall area site is an industrial area and a shopping complex. It is now called Long Binh Ward. I know a number of Vietnam Veterans who took personal trips back to see what South Vietnam looks like today. Several told me that the Long Binh complex is unique and that the local Vietnamese love the American GI's as their forefathers told of their fight to keep and sustain democracy for the South. The history of America's involvement is alive and well!

Richard Nixon was elected president at the start of the 1970's. His campaign promise to the American people was to end the war. Thus, the de-escalation of the Vietnam War became a reality when he entered the White House. The war brought political divisions throughout the United States and was extremely unpopular to the general public.

Long Binh and its allied bases throughout all of South Vietnam were on the horizon of change under President Nixon's leadership. America's war effort in Vietnam was going away.

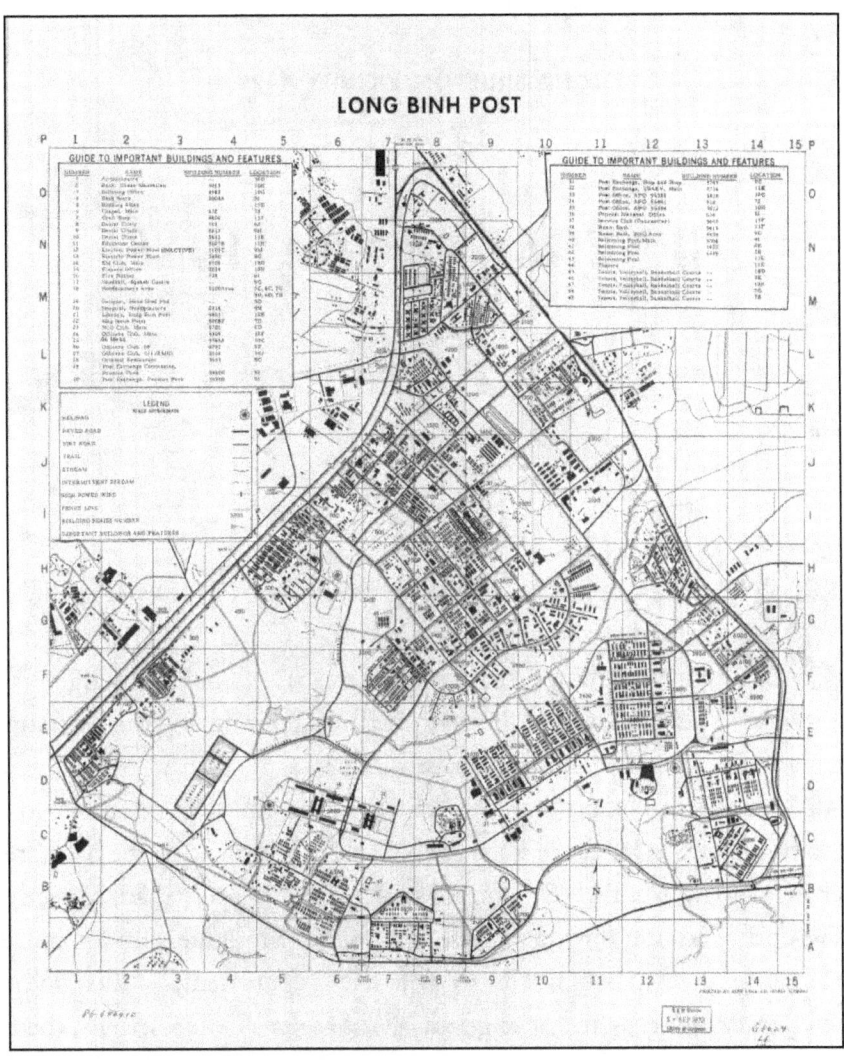

Long Bihn Post: [Vietnam]. [1972?] G8024.L6 1972 .L6 (//lccn.loc.gov/86694410?loclr=blogmap). Library of Congress, Geography & Map Division.

The reverse side of the map depicts Long Binh Post in relation to Saigon. Early in the war, many American units were dispersed throughout Saigon. However, the American command relocated them to Long Binh Post in order to centralize security, logistics, and communications.

GENERAL OPERATIONS

While assigned to the Long Binh Post Fire Department, I served as the Lead Fire Crew Chief (Station Chief) for the assignment of the twenty-one 51M Soldier-Firefighters. "51Mike" was the MOS of the wartime firefighter during the Vietnam era and for several years afterwards.

I was an E-4 Corporal and served as the fire department's Non Commissioned Officer in Charge (NCOIC), reporting to the base fire chief, who was a PA&E contract employee manager. I was directly responsible to him for the twenty 51M soldier-firefighters under me.

During this assignment to the fire department, I was given temporary orders as an "Acting Jack" E-5 Sargent. Unfortunately, there never came available an open slot for me to be promoted to before I left country. I was routinely called "Sarge" or Sargent Kuk, and was given all due NCO respect from the firefighters. This respect was also rendered to me from the Vietnamese fire personnel who replaced us under the PA&E contractor run operation.

As the Station Chief, I was still riding the front seat of the 1st due engine company, Engine 3, and directed my men from that unit. I had plenty of responsibility for a young twenty-one year old soldier in the beginning of all of this, and I took everything extremely serious.

I also had the total responsibility of fire protection supervision for the entire installation, during times when the PA&E chiefs were off duty or away on personal time.

This meant covering five night tours of duty per week, when the PA&E fire chief and assistant chief were off duty. They worked a 56 hour workweek, which required them to pull one twenty-four hour tour of duty per week, that involved bunking in at the main station, with their four eight hours of day tours to flush out their time.

At the main station, both of the 1st due engine companies had five men assigned. The other rigs usually had two men assigned, and the water and foam tenders had a sole driver/operator.

I might add that our firefighters did not enjoy time off from duty, like the traditional 24 hour-on-duty/48 hour-off-duty firefighter work schedule. We were on constant duty except for the one week of R&R which was awarded to all active duty personnel. We were totally quartered at the fire station (24/7/365), and lived there while awaiting calls. We did not have a barracks like other soldiers stationed at Long Binh. Each fire station was the "barracks" for the assigned firefighters. Crew integrity was of keen mission importance to our overall operation.

We were no different in our tour of duty than how the Forward Operating Base (FOB) firefighters worked and lived. These FOB firefighters were also a 24/7/365 group. They were usually a single engine company that protected small operational units and rotary aircraft airfields in remote areas. Their fire apparatus were 530-Bs, and most were painted in the olive drab color scheme, since they were close to the frontlines. Sometimes a surplus 1200 gallon water tender was mated to their operation. Water was a precious commodity to all soldiers, and firefighting was no exception. Fortunately Long Binh did have a well-run water treatment plant.

At Long Binh we were self-contained for basic living needs, and only left the station to use the mess halls and exchange. We took our fire engines with the assigned crew to accomplish these out-bound missions. Thus, i.e., if one firefighter needed to see the dental section, then the whole crew would accompany that firefighter. Crew integrity was paramount in everything we did.

THE FIRE STATIONS

Long Binh had four fire stations on the main cantonment. Station 1 was located at the Main Gate entrance from Highway 1. Station 2 was the airfield. Station 3 was the north side facility, and Station 4 was located in the warehouse district.

It should be noted, that there were six 51M soldier-firefighters independently assigned at the Ammo Dump, who were not part of the overall LBFD operations. Their equipment consisted of a single engine company, a water tender, and a 1-1/4 ton utility. The Ammo Dump firemen were assigned to the Ordnance unit, and never left their designated area of the munitions storage cantonment. If a serious fire occurred at the Ammo Dump, then the LBFD firefighters would respond and directly support the Ammo Dump firefighting crew.

Station 1's crews responded everywhere. These were the firemen that went off post to crashed aircraft, serious military road accidents, POL transport accidents (early HazMat), mutual aid to Saigon Fire Brigade and the Port of Saigon, and even Bien Hoa Air Base. Station 1's crews never knew if they would come back to quarters that day or would be out for unknown periods of time, since some of the calls turned into true extended missions of several days.

Most of the apparatus were quartered outside in the open atmosphere under heavy canvas tarps next to the fire stations. The stations were all constructed of wood, and usually had two to three truck bays to protect some of the first out companies. The apparatus floors were concrete, and the aprons were crushed rock. We had some patches of asphalt for our auxiliary storage sheds.

There was no air conditioning. The sleeping quarters were open bays, and a couple of floor fans were what cooled you off during periods of rest. Mosquito nets were draped above the beds for some protection against the Malaria threat of infection.

We were issued Malaria pills which were taken on Mondays. The medication was very potent and they often interfered with almost everyone's digestive tract.

The typical station layout was as follows: apparatus bay, radio and telephone room, chief's room, storage closet, and sleeping bay. Washroom and restroom facilities were a separate building.

Two daily hot meals were available at a nearby mess hall between the hours of 0530-0700 and 1700-1830.

There was no kitchen facility at the fire stations. We had a couple of refrigerators for our Cokes.

ALARMS, RADIOS, AND DISPATCHING

The main communications office was located in Fire Station 1. Each of the outlying stations had a small desk with a base radio and telephone. There were posted wall maps of Long Binh, and the general area outside the base. A daily journal was kept in the office and of course, a logbook of runs. All of this was well before computers became a daily part of our lives and work.

Of course the fire alarm office was staffed 24/7 by an RTO (Radio Telephone Operator) or other qualified firefighter. Prompt receipt and dispatch of an emergency call was paramount.

Alarms were usually received in three ways. First, the three digit telephone number of 117 directly called the fire department. It was an established number throughout the military branches for fire service response worldwide, both in peacetime and war.

Today's commonplace number of "911" was unheard of back then. Another decade had to pass before this number came into operation for both the military and civilian world to use as the universal standard for emergency response assistance.

The second method was through the MP desk. It would not be uncommon for an MP to be "double-timing" it across the roadway between Station 1 and the MP headquarters office with a slip of paper in his hand of the alarm's incident and location.

The third would be a drive-up. Since cell phones were not invented during that era, it was not unusual for a military vehicle to drive up honking their horn. This usually occurred at night, when the troops with nighttime duties would notice a fire, and quickly drive over to the main station to report the incident.

There were frustrating times for the RTO when he would be unable to get a building number for the emergency. Newly arrived or temporary duty assigned military personnel, who were not familiar with Long Binh, could only give landmark or road-mark descriptions at times.

The RTO did his best to ascertain the approximate location. Sometimes I would run out on the apparatus apron and scan the night sky for a cherry colored glow. As least I got a compass direction by that method to start heading towards what we felt was the emergency's location.

And then there were times when all three of the fire phones started ringing together. We had two "overflow" lines operating, and when these extra phones were ringing, we all knew it was going to be a "working fire."

The main station sat at the main gate (Gate 1) entrance to Long Binh; thus it was a well-known location to most of the soldiers. Telephones were not that commonplace throughout the installation on the roadways. The exception was to go to a command building or a nearby office for calling in an emergency, especially since this was a war zone.

Each communications office had one ringing alarm bell switch to alert the firemen. The exception was at Station 1 where a klaxon horn was also installed and had its own separate switch. The sounding of the klaxon was for a POL response that required the foam apparatus to respond.

The installation did have air raid sirens, which were used to alert all personnel of rocket attacks, but they were controlled by manual activation at command headquarters. These sirens were not of the pre-alert style. They usually were not activated until a good minute or two after the rockets hit the installation. Confirmation and incident location had to be established first.

At Station 1 we did have a PA system, and the announcement of alarms followed the ringing of the bell via this medium. The system was also used for general announcements and operational messages. It sported outside speaker points as well as the station's interior locations.

Station 1's communication office also had two "Handy-Talkies". These were the first portable radios for the fire service. They were invented and built by Motorola, and were quite remarkable for their time.

The Handy-Talkies weighed the full measure of a good sized car battery and then some, as it actually was a modified car battery that powered the device. The base was the battery, and it had a long metal antenna with a telephone style handset to speak into and hear radio borne airwave messages.

One Handy-Talkie was for the PA&E fire chief, with one for the PA&E assistant chief.

The other fire department radios were mounted on a limited number of the apparatus, which were mostly the frontline rigs, and were also built by Motorola. They were of the first generation tube-type, where the radio's tube chassis was installed under the bench seat of the apparatus cab.

The tube chassis was a heavy beast to handle. Whenever the radio chassis needed servicing, it took from anywhere two to four firemen to lift and maneuver the unit from under the bench seat. Their overall weight and bulk were like lifting a boat anchor.

It should be noted that these early vacuum tube units required several minutes to warm up before one could key the microphone and transmit a message. The rig could be about a half a mile from the station before one could use the radio.

These early tube based radios also consumed a lot of electricity to operate. The driver turned the radio on after he started up the engine. It was of extreme importance that he turn the radio off when the apparatus completed its mission. Otherwise the apparatus had a dead battery. Tube based radio chassis severely drained its power source.

Surprisingly, these radios had a remarkable range for their time. One could transmit messages up to 30 miles away from the main station. I don't know if the military used repeater towers for this operational success. We were just happy that they worked and worked well.

FIRE ENGINES AND APPARATUS

Long Binh had a wide variety of apparatus. Some of it was standard issue, some were modified, and some were uniquely constructed for a specific purpose.

I must mention first off that our fire apparatus was painted red. But not a bright traditional red. The red was a true flat red. Basically somewhat subdued, like the military olive drab color for tanks, jeeps, track vehicles, etc. Not one shiny piece on the roster.

The 530-B was the basic unit. It was a true Class A engine with a 400 gallon water tank, 40 gallon foam concentrate tank, 500 gallon-per-minute (GPM) pump, a ladder compliment with either the main ladder being a 24' or 35' extension, 1200 feet of 2-1/2" hose, 400 feet of 1-1/2" hose, dual 1" booster lines, and the usual compliment of hand tools and portable extinguishers.

Some 530-Bs were diesel powered, but the majority was still a multi-fuel gasoline engine. Everything was stick shift and transfer case driven. The electrical system was 24 volt.

Depending upon who the manufacturer was, one would find some differences. Some rigs had single tire rear carriages, while others sported duals. The later diesel engine models had cab stacks, as most employed a ground directed exhaust piping arrangement.

The exhaust was not muffled. The engines were all straight piped. The thinking went back to the days of early motorized fire apparatus. There was to be no restriction to the power plant's generation of horsepower. Thus, by having no restrictions to the release of the exhaust, these engines had a little bit more power and acceleration. Top speed varied between 45-50 mph.

Of course, the noise that was generated was sometimes louder than the sirens. In fact, both the cab and tailboard firefighters used to laugh and tease each other over the roar of which apparatus had the loudest exhaust.

On night time responses one could see the gasoline powered apparatus blowing intermittent sparks and/or a small occasional flame at their respective tailpipe. I guess it was pretty raw and loud after all.

The diesel power plant of the Armored Personnel Carrier (APC) Tank was seriously the loudest of all. Even though the mechanical siren was mounted forward and on the topside front of the Tank, it was easily drowned out by the powerful exhaust.

Overall the 530-B was a very dependable piece of fire apparatus. It could go everywhere, pump forever, and never broke down. This was the military's most widely used fire engine.

Engines 3 and 4 had unique drive trains and transfer cases that permitted these rigs to perform firefighting "pump and roll" operations. Something well ahead of its time to both the military and civilian world of firefighting, at least until the next generation of 530-C apparatus was placed into production and distributed for use by the military.

Chief Petersen had modified the transmission and drive trains of these two 530-Bs with parts from other pieces of military equipment to make this work. He was clever, to say the least, and he enjoyed "hot-rodding" the fire apparatus under his command.

The major names in the manufacture of the 530-B fire engines were Jeep, GMC, American Filter, Ward LaFrance, and a few others. Waterous was the preferred pump, but Hales were also installed.

Long Binh Station 1 had two 530-Bs. Diesel powered Engine 3 was always first out, and considered the structural pumper. It carried protein foam with Rockwood mechanical foam applicator nozzles. It was a single tire tandem chassis.

Engine 4 was also diesel powered and was second due, but responded first to pipeline fires and most of the POL calls. It carried High Expansion Foam concentrate and the large 1-1/2" High-Ex foam nozzles.

High expansion foam was in its infancy at that time, and was highly favored as the class B fire extinguishing agent of choice. It was quite successful on many POL based fires. Since High–Ex foam used very little water to generate large volumes of foam, it was most welcome as the preferred firefighting tool for Class B incidents.

Engine 4 was a dual tired tandem chassis, thus giving it an advantage when going off road to attack pipeline flange fires.

Engine 6 was a 1953 U. S. Navy Federal/General Fire Truck Corporation built open cab Class A with a gasoline engine. It was a very long wheelbase truck that initially came loaded with the Naval standard fire hose that had pipe threaded couplings (National Pipe Thread or NPT).

This was our largest engine and it sported a 750 GPM pump, 100 gallon booster tank, a single booster hose reel, and a very large capacity hose bed. Two thousand feet of 2-1/2" hose was carried in a divided bed. Eight hundred feet of 1-1/2" was also carried, but this small diameter hose sported the NPT couplings, should it be needed to support marine firefighting aboard ocean going vessels.

Engine 6 was positioned outside and covered under a tarp at Station 1, as it was too long to be placed in any of the short apparatus bays.

Tankers 1, 2, 3 and 4 were the Army standard 1200 gallon water tender. They were diesel powered with a dual tandem rear-end on a deuce and a half chassis. A small PTO pump and 1-1/2" supply line fed the 530Bs at fires. The tankers were so numbered to match their assigned stations.

At Stations 1 and 2 there was one "different" tanker. It was also a 1200 gallon tank, but mounted on an International Harvester chassis with a V-8 gasoline engine. It had a small independent gasoline engine powered water pump mounted at the rear. It was painted a Robin's egg blue, but sported a red Beacon Ray light and a mechanical siren, which the local PA&E motor pool crew installed when it became assigned to the fire department.

PA&E procured a large number of these for in-country non-emergency operations when water needed to be trucked in for various projects, like construction or wash-downs. Some of the fire departments received the surplus of the order and left them in their blue color. There was no firefighting equipment carried or mounted otherwise. These were designated as Tankers 6 and 7.

Station 1 did have the sole five thousand gallon tractor-trailer water tender. It was the standard Army 5-ton, attached to its trailered tank ensemble, and had a 300 GPM volume pump mounted midship under the tank. A single 2-1/2" hose was attached to the volume pump for delivery of its water. It was a slow moving vehicle, but provided a large source of water when required. It was designated as Tanker 5.

Unfortunately the service life of the 5-ton tractor of Tanker 5 was shortened in its career. It was stolen by one of the PA&E Vietnamese contract firemen one evening. He unhitched the two units, and quickly drove out the main gate under the cover of darkness. The MP's did not stop him as he drove out, as they thought he was performing official duties. The PA&E fire chief was blistering hot when all of these events unfolded.

Being exceptionally frustrated by this heinous act of treason to the safety of all involved, the PA&E fire chief reached out to several of the villages' police chiefs for assistance.

After all, this large piece of apparatus could also be used to assist at serious village fires that occasionally ravaged the poor population of the local Vietnamese. Eventually he was caught and a regional police chief prosecuted him under their local law. Sadly the 5-ton tractor found its way to the Black Market.

The 5-ton truck never was replaced, and the extra water that Tanker 5 could have brought to a major emergency scene, did create a delay for a sustained water supply.

Foam 1 was a converted POL tanker. It was gasoline powered and constructed much like the standard Army design 1200 gallon water tender. The unit was modified with a transfer pump and hose reel. It carried 6% protein foam pure concentrate. Like the other pieces of apparatus, it sat outside at Station 1 and was used whenever a POL incident occurred.

Foam 2 was another conversion, which was originally a road oil tanker. It had an eight hundred gallon tank and carried the High Expansion foam concentrate tank horizontally. This rig was fitted with the 110 gallon pressurized foam mixing tank for blending the concentrate with incoming water.

Foam 2 carried dual 1-1/2" handlines with the special High-Ex nozzles, and a unique large High-Ex foam generator on the front bumper for large application firefighting. A soft fabric delivery sock or tube could be attached to the large generator, and carried by hand to direct large volumes of finalized foam at a remote point from the apparatus.

A small gasoline engine driven pump provided the delivery of water to the venturi mixing piping and concentrate vessel for operations on Foam 2. It was capable of being a Pump'n'Roll piece of apparatus due to this arrangement of an independent pump being separate from the drive train of the truck. This rig also sat outside at Station 1.

The PA&E fire chief's vehicle was a Dodge pickup truck. Nothing fancy, just a practical vehicle for daily operations and business so required of the position. It carried some basic small tools and portable extinguishers, with mounted radios.

Rescue 1 was the sole piece of rescue apparatus. It carried basic first aid supplies, litters, hand lanterns, the Resuscitator, an assortment of hand tools and manual saws, the Stokes basket, and the cutting torch. A specially mounted oxygen cylinder was installed and fitted with an Inhalator metering valve and delivery mask. This was invaluable for the relief of emergency breathing distress when any of us received too much smoke inhalation. The Rescue was of great benefit to us as a Jeep chassis vehicle. It could go off road, and was invaluable when its tools and hardware needed to be delivered across rough and unstable terrain.

A standard Army Jeep was also on the roster at Station 1. This jeep's rear deck was fitted with the large caliber Multiversal master stream nozzle. It had several open bore tips mounted on the upper rear deck on the jeep and the variable pattern Fog nozzle was always in the mounted position. Of course it sported a siren, and its red warming lights came from surplus parts of the rotary lighting on a junked piece of aircraft.

The most unique piece of apparatus at Station 1 was the "Tank" as everyone called it. It was a converted Armored Personnel Carrier that came from the war scrap pile. The "Tank" was completely rebuilt, including its diesel driven drivetrain. It was originally conceived for fighting ammunition fires, but became more modified for other firefighting challenges.

The APC Tank's crew section was filled with a 900 gallon capacity rubber fuel bladder that was surplus from British fuel transfer operations. The British used these bladders to float on the inland waterways to refuel their equipment. It was also fitted with a fire department connection that ran to a U. S. Navy P-250 portable pump.

The APC Tank was capable of delivering three mediums of extinguishing agents via a valved "Waterthief" three-way appliance that was connected to the P-250 pump. First there was water from the

900 gallon rubber bladder, followed by 90 gallons of High-Ex foam concentrate carried in the rear-mounted mixing vessel, and then two fifty-five gallon drums of 6% foam concentrate that were mounted on top of the APC's deck.

A short fifteen foot section of 1-1/2" hose was attached to one outlet of the Waterthief. The other two outlets fed either the High-Ex system or the O-11A crash truck foam nozzle.

What was unique here is that the High-Expansion foam was delivered via a large capacity nozzle that was carried on a boom arm. The boom could be extended and maneuvered where it was most effective in delivering foam over the earthen mounds that protected the ammo storage points.

The boom was extended and flowed its foam when fighting wooden ammo boxes and/or pallets that caught fire from enemy attack at the ammo dump. It could quickly smother the fires with the High Expansion foam before the fires grew in intensity and caused the ammunition to go high order. Since earthen walls were built around the stored ammo, the boom with its extension capabilities could be brought into play for extinguishment.

During its responses the APC Tank was operated by two firefighters. One was the driver, and the other was the dual role commander and actual firefighter who had his choice of weapons to use. The Tank was always 1st due at the Ammo Dump, whenever the LBFD main station was notified of an alarm there.

The last piece of equipment quartered at Station 1 was an open bed tracked vehicle, similar to the APC Tank. Although it was not on the LBFD roster as such, it was assigned on long-term loan from the Engineer motor pool for our "hot-work" requirements. It was identified as the "Track".

The Track carried the Napalm generator tank, gas pressure system, and flame throwers for the burning operations. This flame-throwing tracked unit was accompanied by the Tank during these missions. The Tank was used for the overall control of any spreading fire.

Neither the APC Tank nor the open-bed Track vehicle were assigned an LBFD number for unit identification. The firefighting APC was always called the "Tank", and the open-bed Track Vehicle was simply called the "Track".

Fire Station 2 was the Crash station, and some novel equipment was quartered there for the specific challenges of aircraft crash-fire-rescue protection.

The most unique piece of apparatus was a dual engine 530-B crash wagon. Since Chief Petersen did not have a true crash truck to chase aircraft with, he went on to design, and build his own.

He took a spare gasoline engine from a scrapped 2-1/2 ton truck, and mounted it sideways above the pump area of that 530-B. It became directly connected to the fire pump and remained independent of the engine that propelled the rig. Thus, it could "pump and roll" anywhere on the tarmac.

Firefighting foam and water could be easily delivered while the vehicle was in motion, and that's what a true crash unit was supposed to do.

This home-made Crash Wagon/Foam Engine had an unusual circular tank mounted above the pump area. The irregular superstructure provided for additional water and foam concentrate capacity, which would be needed if a large frame aircraft were on fire.

This home-made crash wagon was given the designation of Engine 1 for the LBFD roster.

Station 2 also had a traditional 530-B for protection of its structures, which mainly consisted of the Quonset hut style buildings. The Quonsets were sturdy and afforded good shelter from the elements, in particular the heavy rains. This 530-B was set up to match the other stations' structural apparatus.

For water tender support, an Army 1200 gallon deuce and a half tender was stationed there as Tanker 2. The second of the two blue commercial International Harvester tankers was also kept there. It was set up identical to Station 1's rig, and assigned the radio sign Tanker 7.

Station 2's jeep was unique and the only one-of-its-kind piece of apparatus on Long Binh. It had a canvas top to shield the two man crew and its hardware, but sported a CB tank with a hose reel. This jeep also carried an Ansul extinguisher mounted horizontally on its right rear deck.

The jeep's tank carried CB, or Chlorobromomethane, which was a halongenated agent that offered considerable success in fighting flammable liquid fires under the right conditions and application. CB quickly converted into a gas upon application against a fire.

This jeep had an eighty gallon tank powered by a nitrogen cylinder. Opening the valve on the nitrogen cylinder forced the CB into the hose reel, and then a firefighter could direct the stream with a valved nozzle unto the fire.

CB was still a fairly new extinguishing agent for firefighting use against exotic fuels. It was developed by the German Navy for use on WWII war vessels against engine room fires, and in particular, for injection into confined spaces of ocean-going ships where diesel fuel was in use and/or stored.

It was ideal for literally "smothering" a fire within a confined space. The U.S. Air Force started using this chemical gas because of its cleaner agent attributes around the early 1950's with good results. Thus, the rest of the military fire services followed suit for aircraft requirements.

Station 3 was the North station and it protected troop housing. At one time Engine 6, the Federal, was stationed there, before it came to Station 1.

The roster for Station 3 consisted of two 530-Bs, one Deuce and a half 1200 gallon water tender, and one jeep. Just basically a fundamental structural department, with nothing fancy or unique. Station 3's vehicular equipment were simple "work-horse" apparatus.

Station 4 was located within the warehouse compound. It had a single engine company and that was because of the inner fully looped hydrant system. Water tender support was not needed.

The sole engine stationed within the warehouse district was a vintage 1942 Mack, and it was given the fire company designation of Engine 8. It was essentially a city type of rig, and it had no indicators that it was built for any type of foreign war demands. Given its age, it was probably rapidly built and procured by the military in the early days of WWII as it rolled off the Mack assembly line in Allentown, for its assignment to protect military assets at Fort Hood.

The Mack had a pumping capacity of 600 gallons per minute. It only contained 100 gallons of water in its booster tank, but carried 1500 feet of 2-1/2" hose with an assortment of nozzles. This made it ideal for service within the warehouse compound with available hydrants for water supply. It was also a short wheelbase truck, thereby permitting it to navigate the narrow passageways of the warehouses more easily.

I am going make an improved and detailed mention of our nearest U. S. Army firefighting brothers, the 114th Engineer Firefighting Detachment. Although they were not a permanent party of Long Binh's tenants, they were a small department that protected Fire Support Bases Mace and Buttons, and the large ordnance supply point, which was known as Long Binh Ammo Dump.

The Dump was north of us in a somewhat remote sector, obviously constructed there for a number of safety reasons. The 114th stayed busy on their own during their time in country, being constantly on fire watches, patrols, and general fire prevention activities. After all, they had some serious major responsibility in the course of their assigned mission for ordnance protection. Anything overlooked would compromise lives and the war mission.

They had a basic roster of three pieces of apparatus. These were a 530-B engine, a Dodge chassis 1000 gallon water tender, and a 1-1/4 ton utility 4x4. There were six firefighters assigned to their mission.

I must mention about our warning devices for alerting traffic during our response. Red lens beacon ray lights, and mechanical sirens were the norm. The sole exception was Engine 3 which sported a blue lens beacon ray light atop the cab. European emergency vehicles used a blue lens color instead of red as their color of warning for emergency response.

Just about all of the apparatus did have mounted sirens. We hardly ever used them, except when to pass other vehicles when we encountered them on the roadways.

Since our apparatus was painted red, we were very visible, and usually granted the right-of-way.

Believe it or not, but PA&E had a boneyard for vehicles. Numerous pieces of fire apparatus were in that collection. There was a wide assortment of apparatus, and each piece looked like it could tell a unique story by the condition it was in. We would sometimes go there and reclaim some parts for our trucks.

The yard was guarded and one had to have authorization to obtain parts. Since PA&E employed some of the local nationals as security guards, they all had a price for admitting one into the area, and procuring whatever one needed.

Usually a carton or cartons of cigarettes could get you whatever you wanted. Since I did not smoke, I would use my ration card for cigarettes, and make the deal. Everyone was happy.

The items that we usually needed were light bulbs, nozzles, fittings, window glass, and minor truck repair components that we couldn't get fast enough via the motor pool channels. We found it faster and better for us to make our own repairs, and ensure that the job was done right!

APPARATUS EXHAUST AND THE STATION'S ENVIRONMENT

The way in which the fire stations were constructed back then for the military left many negative elements towards our living conditions, especially with no air conditioning.

First of all, there were no solid doors anywhere in the main structure. Everything was wide open, and one could venture anywhere easily with only a single screen door entrance to the sleeping area and the alarm room. Basically a very simple floor plan was it.

It appeared to work well for us transgressing the confines of the station in response to an alarm and other required duties. That was essentially it…no benefit otherwise to our life, our privacy, nor our security in a fire station's quarters from any outside negative activity.

When the apparatus got started, our breathing atmosphere changed quickly from the effects and emissions of the apparatus exhaust. The exhaust immediately entered every space of the station.

No one could escape the lingering smell of the engines. The two diesels of Engines 3 and 4 were sooty and foul smelling, to say the least. And on days with rain, we pump tested our rigs inside the apparatus bays. More negative atmosphere was generated in conducting our daily routine!

Unless a good breeze was blowing crossways to the station, these toxic odors hung around for a good while.

Given what we know today, we were all exposed to the potential carcinogenic results of inhaled diesel exhaust. No one of us understood the direct poisoning of diesel emission fumes.

Sad to say, but after a while, we all became accustomed to it.

FIRE HOSE AND NOZZLES

The fire hose was the traditional double jacket cotton with a rubber lining. A typical 50' section of 2-1/2" weighed close to 90 lbs. It all had to be cleaned and dried after use. The goose-egging of brass couplings had to be tended to at times also. The 1-1/2" hose was constructed in the same manner.

The 1" Booster hose was the thick-walled rubber constructed hand line. Fortunately it was carried on hose reels that were equipped with electric motors for windup. Most booster reels were still hand-cranked, and when one was dead tired after a serious fire, the last thing you wanted to do was to perform more manual labor.

The nozzles were all brass and some were chrome plated. The Navy fog nozzle with applicators of various lengths were standard issue. PA&E did purchase some of the more popular fog nozzles that were making their rounds in the states, such as the Santa Rosa or the Akron Brass "Mystery Nozzle", as they offered a more dense fog pattern than the Navy droplet style did.

High Expansion nozzles were also purchased and carried on specific apparatus.

There was one master stream "Multiversal" that had several different sized open bore tips and one variable pattern fog nozzle. It was of a 1250 GPM maximum flow rate capacity.

The hard suction sleeves were of the standard "Steamer" design in a ten foot length. They sported 4-1/2" National Standard Threads (NST) and couplings.

All of the hose threads were NST made for the mutual aid benefit between any American military firefighting unit, permitting all firehose couplings to mate immediately with each other. There was a limited supply of 1-1/2" hose that had NPT because it was carried for use when the LBFD responded to mutual aid fires at Saigon Docks. These Naval connections were of the common pipe thread standard. Engine 6 had the loaded compliment of the NPT fire hose, and was the primary marine response company, which was usually staffed by Engine 3's personnel.

WATER SUPPLY

Water for most firefighting operations had to be carried. The department roster had four 1200 gallon Army fuel tenders on the deuce and a half chassis, which were adapted for fire service requirements. These were diesel powered, and had small PTO pumps of 60 or 90 GPM. A single open butt 1-1/2" hose line was used to refill the tank inlet tray on the 530-Bs.

A large 5000 gallon tank unit with a tractor-trailer 5 ton was the sole big water mover for the LBFD initially, until it got stolen.

When major fires occurred, the LBFD alarm operator (RTO) called for post wide water tender support from the various military units. A literal flood of 5 ton tractors with their 5000 gallon tanks would come to off-load their potable water to any fire engine needing support. It worked very well.

The lone exception for a true fire hydrant water supply system was exclusively in the warehouse compound. This high value area had an underground looped fire water main system with approximately fifty hydrants located throughout the warehouse compound's confines.

This sole system was fed by dual diesel driven fire pumps feeding off of a two million gallon reservoir. There was a small "jockey" fire pump that maintained a steady pressure of approximately sixty pounds on the loop. Once the pressure dropped, then the two large pumps kicked in for the firefighting mode.

The water treatment plant ran a two inch line over to the fire water reservoir for re-supply purposes. Obviously, this feeder line could not keep up with any serious depletion of the master reservoir during an extended fire water demand. This small line was to assist in maintaining a full reservoir before a major fire struck the warehouse compound.

Having a true fire hydrant system for the protection of our critical warehouse compound was of paramount importance. When we had fires here, it was extremely reassuring that a dependable supply of water would be available to us for firefighting and suppression.

RESCUE AND MEDICAL EQUIPMENT

As one looks back in time, there is a vast difference in all of the equipment that was carried on 1970's era apparatus. Some of it is still a part of today's necessary hardware, and some of today's gear was not invented in that timeframe.

All of our rescue tools were hand operated. These were wood saws, hacksaws, crowbars, pry bars, a Jimmy tool, axes, and a toolbox full of everything from screwdrivers to wrenches.

We also had five ton and ten ton hydraulic jacks for lifting. A four ton Porto-Power set was also carried, which was basically an auto body shop device that was used for pushing and pulling metal. The rescue sported a Stokes basket and couple of Army issued folding stretchers.

We carried a pair of heavy duty log chains which we used for head-on collisions, and different entrapment accidents. They worked well for us when we encountered these challenges.

The log chains were slipped through or around the area of a vehicle that needed to be opened up. Usually the seating points. Then the chains were secured to the front bumper U-hooks of two fire engines, that were positioned front and back of the wrecks, which needed to be pulled apart.

Once this was completed, then the signal for both engines to back up were given. Slowly there would be enough force created to pull-apart the vehicles, and give us access for removing the victims.

Our "heaviest" extrication tool was the cutting torch. Most of the accidents and rescue incidents involved metallic vehicles. Thus the torch worked well, but we had to be patient, as it took time to cut through the various thickness of metallic vehicles.

And we had to be extra diligent since this was an open flame process. Pulling the booster and having the dry chemical extinguishers or the CO_2's at the ready were an absolute necessity to extinguish any fire startup.

If we encountered spilled fuel, then a foam blanket was laid on the ground, and re-applied as often as required. The hot sun was unforgiving in destroying the foam cover via the ultraviolet rays of the daytime sunbeams.

Our first aid kits were just that. Basic first aid with splinting material. All of us were trained in the American Red Cross eight hour first aid course. That was the defined standard of the day.

Our kits had assorted bandages and related material for dressing war injuries. We took whatever the medics gave us, and we were happy to have something to stock our kits.

Our most sophisticated piece of medical hardware was the Pressure-Cycle Resuscitator/Inhalator. It weighed in at around ninety pounds, and was "the" oxygen delivery device of its day.

It sported dual size D oxygen cylinders that actually drove the cycling of the resuscitator, and delivered pure oxygen via the mask. One had to insert the correct size of one of the chrome-plated metallic airways into a non-breathing patient. Then one performed a jaw-lift maneuver with the mask to start the resuscitator into its repetitive cycling.

If properly worked by a good technician, one could actually see the rise and fall of a patient's chest. It was successful on anyone who still had a heartbeat and was in respiratory failure, but it did nothing for a full arrest. CPR was not being taught out in the field at that time, nor was it even heard of outside of an emergency or operating room setting.

There was one change-over valve on the resuscitator that converted it into an Inhalator. By moving this valve, the flow of oxygen would bypass the pressure-cycle mechanism, and flow into the mask. Then the mask could be held to one's face and they could freely breathe in fresh oxygen. The delivered oxygen was metered in several flow measurements and did offer some relief until one was seen by a higher medical authority.

The Inhalator function was ideal for the temporary relief and recovery of what the "Smoke-Eaters" had to endure in the performance of their duties in smoke-laden atmospheres. Too much smoke usually resulted in severe headaches, dizziness, and vomiting for all of us. Any rapid delivery of concentrated oxygen to overcome firefighters was paramount first aid for recovery.

This unit did sport a suction device. Unfortunately it consumed vast amounts of oxygen when it was used. There was a Venturi throat that took the high pressure of the flowing oxygen to create a suction effect through an attached tube.

The tube's suction tip nozzle was actually too small in diameter to evacuate any large pieces of vomit, which usually occurred during most cardiac events. We also did not care to use it because of the large consumption of precious oxygen during its operation.

FIRE FIGHTING FOAM, AFFF, AND OTHER EXTINGUISHING AGENTS

One thing that the Army made sure of, was that we had plenty of firefighting foam concentrate. And the principal commodity was the foul smelling protein foam of 6% strength. National Foam was the major producer here for the Army during this timeframe.

We had multiple stacks of five gallon protein foam concentrate everywhere. It was stacked an average of five to seven cans high between our apparatus on the bay floors and apparatus apron. Of course, some of the 530-Bs had their forty gallon foam tanks filled with it.

What we discovered with the protein foam's stability or instability, was that a breakdown of a foam blanket easily occurred in direct sunlight. If we established a protective foam blanket over a POL spill or accident, then we were usually re-applying another blanket of foam throughout the incident, as the sun continued to shine.

We did have some cans of Merlefoam. This concentrate was made with an inhibitor that resisted the ultra-violet rays of direct sunlight.

But unfortunately, we had very limited supplies. It was kept for use to protect high value military assets.

The high expansion foam concentrate was also well stocked. The brand name was simply called "High-Ex". Whenever one opened a five gallon container, it would feel like inhaling the vapors after a big splash of Dawn dish soap got spilled. The department's "chemists" all chimed in that we were using dish soap to kill fires! I think they were right...

The High-Ex concentrate could be inducted in any percentage from 1% to 10% strength to make suitable fire suppression foam. Most of the time, we stayed at a 2% concentration for ordinary firefighting efforts. It would get kicked up to 3% or 6% for some of the POL situations, if the foam's bubbles were breaking up when they hit the fire's surface.

In the 1970's the military fire service was introduced to a new type of firefighting foam. It was invented by a scientist by the name of Irving Langmuir. Scientist Langmuir originated the concept of surface-active liquids for the foam industry with research scientist Dr. Richard Tuve and their United States Navy Fire Research Team in 1962. A real landmark invention!

It was in late November 1970 that the LBFD PA&E Fire Chief E. L. Petersen and I were invited to Bien Hoa airbase for a demonstration of this "new" type of firefighting foam called Aqueous Film Forming Foam (AFFF). In our ride over there we discussed the fact that this was already making a mark in several of the stateside bases, and that the USAF crash rigs were being loaded with this concentrate. We were anxious to see it first-hand.

Upon our arrival we were greeted and given a brief explanation of what was to take place. We looked at the five gallon buckets of concentrate and noticed that it required a 6% setting on the foam meters and eductors. We also smelled the solution, and noticed that it was not anything like the animal based protein odor that we were so used to.

The demonstration consisted of two pits, and each was to hold approximately two-hundred gallons of JP-4 jet fuel. They were simple open flat pits with no metal objects or obstructions, like those found at a training facility with a mock fuselage of an aircraft.

Two teams of firefighters, suited in their "Silvers", were going to extinguish the burning pits after a two minute burn time elapsed. Both teams were a two man ensemble. One crew was going to use the standard issue 6% concentrate protein foam and the second team was to use the new AFFF, also at a 6% concentration.

The moment came and the pits were lit. A hot steady fire engulfed both pits, and everything was burning freely when the signal for the application of the foam was given.

Almost immediately the AFFF crew was knocking down the fire, and pushing it to a rapid course of extinguishment. The protein foam team had secured about two feet of coverage when the AFFF crew nearly had their pit extinguished.

The AFFF crew was starting to "plunge" their stream into a deeper part of the pit's fuel, as they were trying to kill the last surface area of the fire, and that's when Dr. Tuve stepped in. He was in his street clothes, and shouted some advice to the firefighters about directing the foam stream across the surface, and to not aim it into the pool of fuel.

His advice worked, as they were able to completely kill the fire. The protein firefighters were only about a fourth of the way towards making a secure blanket to work the fire.

Thus, this demonstration gave hope that the future of firefighting foam was going to change, and that a more rapid knockdown of fuel based fires involving aircraft would save lives.

Halogenated extinguishing agents were still being used in various degrees and amounts at many installations. Long Binh was no exception.

The old and now forbidden Carbon Tetrachloride (CCL4) extinguisher fluid was the earliest developed halogenated extinguishing agent. It was an effective agent, whereby it produced a chlorinated methane gas that robbed the atmosphere of oxygen. When the agent came into direct contact with an open flame, it quickly converted into Phosgene gas. The Phosgene vapors and fumes are what snuffed out the fire, and could also take firemen's lives in the process.

A large number of these extinguishers were located throughout any given military installation, despite legislation being passed in the 1950's to stop using this as an extinguishing agent.

When this extinguishing agent was deployed, the result was that the fire was basically "choked" to death. CCL4 basically removed life sustaining oxygen from the atmosphere.

The negative sidebar to this agent was that a number of firefighters and civilians also suffered serious inhalation injuries, and/or death, since they were in a negative zone of absent oxygen and lung tissue destroying chlorinated vapors.

Carbon Tetrachloride was effective in aircraft piston engine nacelles, and it continued to be used until stricter measures became enforced. The upside to using this agent was that it left literally no residue, and that cleanup and restoration was much easier to perform after a dirty fire.

As I mentioned earlier, LBFD did have Station 2's jeep fitted with a single large capacity CB (Chlorobromomethane) tank for quick response crash firefighting. The CB contained a mixture of chlorine and bromine as the principal forces for making this an extinguishing agent.

CB was developed by the Germans and used for extinguishing fires in the holds of ships, being especially effective on fuel oil based fires. Thus, it was also used against aircraft fires with good success.

We never did use the CB during any of our firefighting incidents. It was quite expensive as a suppression agent, and it was somewhat rare to obtain via either the military supply channels or PA&E's procurement process. Thus, it was looked at as a "last resort measure".

HAUNTING HEALTH ISSUES FROM THE EXTINGUISHING AGENTS

Today many, if not all, of the military and contract civilian firefighters who used the above mentioned extinguishing agents are now suffering from health issues related to these chemicals. What was unknown to us at that time is now being discovered, and the results are very negative.

The AFFF fire foam concentrate is becoming the new "Tsunami" that is affecting a large number of us. Since the Air Force firefighters used and were in contact with this product daily, more than the other military firefighters, they have led the pack on health challenges.

Many have died at young ages because of this exposure. Several vendors have stopped selling and making this type of foam concentrate because it is now very well-known of the far reaching negative health effects.

In 20/20 hindsight, we should have picked up on the corrosive nature of the concentrate, whereas the foam storage tanks on our apparatus would quickly start rusting out while the chemical was being stored there.

We had to have stainless steels tanks replace the ordinary carbon steel units usually within a couple of months after filling these with the AFFF.

Thus, one can imagine what our respiratory systems were exposed to whenever we were inhaling these fumes and vapors, especially during the refilling process. Of course, we splashed this chemical occasionally on our skin and clothing, without giving it a second thought.

There were no warnings on the drums and containers of the concentrate. Just our military stock code and the words "Aqueous Film Forming Foam".

At no time did we ever receive instruction that this firefighting chemical was of concern to us and our overall health. It was championed as one of the most fantastic inventions for us to have in our firefighting arsenal. It worked and that's all that we were concerned with at that time.

Numerous articles are being published about the health history here, and Internet chat rooms and social media is alive with discussion from all involved. It's a true serious health concern.

This battle is far from over for some of us.

MESS, FOOD AND DRINK

Hot meals...not every day did the firemen enjoy such a treat. If we were out on calls, then you had either a C-Ration that was carried in an upper compartment on the rig, or ate some food that your loved ones sent you when you got back to your assigned station. My folks were great about sending Rye-Crisp. It was excellent to sustain you until you had something more substantial.

There were times when we went without food until the next day. Especially if the C-Ration selections were not your favorite. And, if you ate too much smoke from a fire, then one usually avoided food intake, and preferred a drink like Coca-Cola. Eating after any smoke inhalation episode sometimes brought on stomach upsets, which resulted in vomiting.

Sometimes we cooked on our homemade grill, which was half of an abandoned 55 gallon drum. No one gave it a thought as to what chemical residue remained impregnated in the metal. We just wanted to eat.

The potable water was treated, so we did have some level of safe water on a daily basis. Most of us drank Cokes and used the water for showers, brushing your teeth, washing the apparatus, and refilling the water tanks of the apparatus, as the water's odor was annoying.

I believe this is where my love for Coca-Cola started. Although I have tried to slow down my consumption these past couple of years, I still drink too much Coca-Cola daily.

Beer was either the Black Label and Lone Star brands. In the evening some personnel quietly drank a beer after a meal, and no one got drunk. Our lives depended upon each other, and being in a stupor was not part of our duty as soldier-firemen in a war zone.

Going to the mess halls was a treat, as getting some fresh hot food before the bells rang again, was quite a morale booster. Overall the food was tasteless, but it had nourishment.

If we were out on early morning runs, and the time was around 3 am, then one of the trucks would swing by the installation bakery. The cooks there would give us several loaves of fresh bread to take back. It was hot and fresh, and was like a candy bar treat to us. There was no preservatives used. The bread had to be made daily, since the normal atmospheric weather of South Vietnam quickly destroyed the integrity of the bread within several hours.

But it was not what it all seemed. There were long periods when we had nothing to eat because we were working extended serious emergencies and missions. And sometimes one was just too fatigued to eat. A constant diet of C-Rations was not appealing after time.

I was in excellent physical condition when I came in country. I was built solid with plenty of muscle and weighed 168 lbs. I mustered out at 127 lbs. During my time there I lost 41 lbs. We were all beat up by the constant runs and lack of a proper diet. One of the last photos taken of me before I left Vietnam clearly showed my physique of "spaghetti" arms, and a thin face.

I mentioned drinking cokes earlier. The French, with local national Vietnamese employees, operated a Coca-Cola bottling plant just north of Saigon right off of Highway 1. We stopped there when returning from off-post runs as often as we could, especially after helping Saigon

Brigade at dock fires or POL blazes that required our foam and specialized apparatus.

The Vietnamese employees always gave us free cases of Coke because they knew that we helped protect their villages from fires when their little fire brigades were overwhelmed or had no other protection. Our 530-Bs looked like hay wagons upon entering the main cantonment. There were wooden cases with glass bottles of Coke stacked high upon the hose beds!

And to top all of this off, they still used real cocaine root in the soda makeup. When one would pop the metal cap, the fizz to your nose was very real. No wonder we all came alive after a refreshing bottle of Coca-Cola!

On a couple of holidays we would receive a case of steaks from Command. So we cooked them on our fabricated charcoal grills from discarded chemical and/or POL drums. And no one knew about what harmful chemical or residue might have been in the drum prior to our using it.

Charcoal for our home-made grills was easily available to us from one of the small village shops. The Vietnamese used open flame cooking and grilles to prepare their food daily, and charcoal was an affordable fuel for them.

Overall, this was like a touch of home for us, to grill and enjoy a respite from everything.

THE SOLDIER-FIREFIGHTERS

A special brotherhood of men made up our roster. Like I made mention before, this wartime firefighter MOS of 51M required the 11-Bravo qualifications first for our selection into the Special Troops assignment to the Long Binh Fire Department. And one needed to be in the top 10% tier of the AIT graduates, if one expected to be selected for this MOS.

Not everyone initially had an MOS of 51M when they first arrived at the fire department. Some of the apparatus drivers were former concrete truck specialists, heavy equipment operators, and convoy truck drivers. The alarm operator was an RTO from a field unit. Most of us were AIT 11-Bravo (Light Weapons Infantry) qualified, and since I had stripes from the NCO academy, I became the fire crew chief.

I was an 11-Bravo with Corporal rank, and with my stateside auxiliary firefighting background, I became the lead fire crew chief, which really equated to being the station fire chief for overall operations. In serving as station fire chief, I was the military detachment leader (aka military fire chief), reporting to the PA&E fire chief.

There never was a discipline problem within our ranks. We all got along, and became good friends during our time together. And we were a true mix of American society. White, Black, and Hispanic were our backgrounds. We looked at each other as soldier-firefighters in a special blend of brotherhood. Each of us were very proud to serve together in this unique and extremely limited MOS.

The alarms and assignments that we went on were extremely diverse for that point in time. We exercised innovative operational methods to save life and property back then. Everyone had raw courage. As I reflect back, this small detail of LBFD Firefighters were clever, brave, and daring.

Unfortunately we were of low rank within the fire department. Only the truck drivers and RTO were Specialist 4s. I was the sole hard stripe Corporal as the NCOIC. Everyone else was of E-2 or E-3 rank.

Overall the soldier-firefighters in-country were not truly unified in structure and assignment. Thus, that probably explains the low level of rank and pay, and duty station placement. And why none of us would consider staying in the Army, having this as your primary MOS. Extremely limited opportunities for a higher pay grade and overall promotions!

It was uneven throughout all of Vietnam for assignments that required firefighters. Most Army firefighters were usually assigned to Aviation and Ordnance units and detachments. There were a few Quartermaster firefighters assigned in various places too, usually consisting of a small detachment that protected supply points and warehousing. Something of a shadow of their WWII lineage. In our case, we were the only group of firefighters ever assigned to Special Troops. We were hand-picked, and enjoyed a special status on the installation.

As Special Troop Firefighters, we did everything that Army Command required of us, and that included extremely dangerous and hazardous missions that no one else could undertake.

Despite being on the same installation, Long Binh firefighters were a permanent section of the USARV Special Troops, while the Ammo Dump firefighters were assigned to Ordnance.

Funny thing, once we were sent to the fire department, we never saw our immediate Army chain of command again, unless they showed up at a serious incident or major fire, and we did not know about it. They left us alone, which I feel was a compliment.

Only once did our CO, a young 1st Lieutenant, come to see us from his headquarters in Saigon. The ranking E-6 fire inspector came by once also. He was basically the NCO who went to all of the FOBs to ensure that things were in order at this myriad of forward and front line small bases.

Again, there was very little upper rank structure for Army firefighting personnel during our time in Vietnam. Promotions basically did not exist. There were simply no slots for anyone to promote to, much less entertain this MOS as a military life path career after the war.

In fact some of us came home on orders cut on the financial resources of another MOS, just to pay the costs of getting us stateside. Crazy how limited money was for the firefighters! I guess we were an abstract to the finance section.

Of course, there were several Army recruiters' desks on location, of which we had to pass by on our exit from the out-processing facility. They were there to give us "one last chance" of reconsidering a career in the Army. Most of us (all Vietnam veterans now) quickly "double-timed" as we passed the desks. Pretty much everyone had enough of the Army life in Vietnam. I had one recruiter, a senior NCO, call out to me, and so I stopped and listened to him.

The recruiter noted that I was a firefighter, and he said that the Army always has great respect for our MOS. Well, that really caught my attention! Thus, he went on to tell me that I could be made a hard-stripe E-5 today, and within six months be promoted to E-6. Wow, I thought what's going on here!

He explained that there was limited rank and structure to remain in the Army firefighting career, and I already knew that, so what he said to me next did take me by surprise.

The recruiter said for me to change my MOS of Firefighting to EOD. EXPLOSIVE ORDANCE DISPOSAL! Those words were nowhere in my young mind. I was stuck in my tracks at that moment. And I paused for several minutes, and then took a chair next to his desk. I sat down, and I went into a deep thought, and actually felt pretty "cool" about that offer.

This senior NCO kept on selling me about how the Army knows that firefighters were brave and daring, and yet could work very hazardous events with a great outcome. He said we displayed calm thinking and were practical performers in a variety of skills. Thus, according to him, we were ideal candidates for EOD.

He was really convincing overall, and I started having second thoughts about leaving the Army behind. Then my memory kicked in and reminded me that things were waiting for me back home. Music and a civil service career were the advent at my doorstep.

I told him that these two careers were on the horizon already and I thanked him for his time and explanation. He said that I could muster back in within the month if I changed my mind. I just had to visit a local recruiting office.

CUU HOA

One item of particular note is that the translation for firefighter or fire department in the Vietnamese language was "Cuu Hoa". It was painted on the left field of the Maltese Cross emblems that adorned our apparatus, and it was heard whenever we encountered the Vietnamese talking about us.

Whenever we came into a close encounter with the local Vietnamese, usually passing by or purchasing a drink, there was always a warm reception. Sometimes it was a friendly smile, a nod or a bow, and a verbal expression of "Cuu Hoa is # 1!". The local people knew that the Army soldier-firefighters were there to help, and this was their way to let us know that we were appreciated. It really did lift our spirits when these moments took place.

Of course, whenever we went to a village or hamlet fire, and did some good work in stopping a raging blaze, the inhabitants let us know what they thought of us as our apparatus departed. We were hailed with a mixture of sincere gratitude indeed! There was cheering, waving hands, and a chorus of voices with clapping as we left the location after taking up when the fire was out.

As I look back in time, while reflecting upon those fleeting moments of doing the job, I now have a vivid memory of how poor these folks were in a war zone. And when their meager possessions and homes were going up in smoke, I fully understand what we meant to them by showing up and fighting these fires, as most did not have any sort of organized firefighting assets.

THE DRUG ENVIRONMENT

One common discussion back in the States about the Vietnam War was that drugs were easily available to all of us at any time. I will have to agree in the affirmative that this statement was true. But the fact remains that the vast majority of the in-country soldiers did not participate in the use of drugs, at least not from what I saw.

There were numerous sources to obtain marijuana or "pot" as it was commonly called during that timeframe. Other drugs of the "hard" variety were also available from local nationals and/or the Black Market. Although it was not open discussion, certain individuals were known to be sources for illegal contraband. Quiet encounters usually produced whatever one wanted for a price. The Black Market could be used for obtaining anything, if you had cold hard cash.

Fortunately, drugs did not enter our fire stations. The soldier-firefighters were indifferent to the use of drugs. There were a few discussions amongst some members about their trying pot when still in high school, and they considered beer and hard liquor to be a better choice for relaxing and enjoying themselves. Most also did not want any trouble with the law back then, as any form of drug involvement could have long term jail sentences. We all wanted Honorable Discharges when we mustered out.

OFF POST RESPONSE AND SECURITY

We did respond off post whenever we were called. Basically we were provided with an MP gun jeep with a .50 caliber ahead of us, and one behind if available. This was a standard escort that the MPs tried to maintain. The MPs were a great bunch of guys too. They were like us, plenty to do all the time to protect and maintain security of the installation, and keep the peace.

These escorts were sometimes beefed up with the MPs furnishing an extra jeep if we had a small convoy of apparatus responding to a critical incident.

There were a few times when the MPs could not provide an escort, and so we went alone. We were assigned steel helmets, flak vests, and M-14 full automatic rifles, including .45 caliber pistols. We always wore the .45 calibers under our turnout gear.

It's interesting to note that we were the only MOS to be assigned dual weapons from the arms room, which consisted of .45 pistols and M-14 full automatic rifles. We were to always keep our side arms on us at all times, even while fighting fire, under out turnout coats. The

M-14s stayed with the driver/operator locked up on the apparatus during firefighting or rescue operations.

If the installation came under attack, and we were all in quarters, then the fifth man of each engine company would drop off of the rig and go to our assigned pillbox. He would serve as a long gun to the MPs. Most of our M-14's had modified scopes with the night vision technology of that timeframe, which came in handy when we were manning our pillbox for watch duties.

WEATHER AND FIRES

Our average daily temperature at Long Binh was approximately 103 degrees. When the monsoon season arrived we got some relief to the heat, but there was a downside to that.

The monsoon rains were very dense at times and visibility was near zero. Even in the daytime, we experienced radical situations in going to emergency calls. These monsoon runs were a severe challenge in any form or manner of conducting a quick and rapid response to a call.

Many times I got out of the front seat of the rig, turned on my hand lantern and directed it back to the truck, so the driver/operator could see me. Then I walked ahead of the engine to ensure that we stayed on the roadway. Some of the roads were narrow with ditches on either side.

It also seemed like we always had an electrical fire during any outburst of the monsoon rains. When the rains started getting fierce, most of us went to our apparatus, and awaited the forthcoming alarms. We were usually partially dressed in our PPE, ready to roll out.

A FIRE AT THE 24TH EVAC

We had a smoky job at the 24th EVAC hospital during one downpour from a monsoon sweeping over the area. An AC wall unit got grounded, and then broke into a lazy flame from the electrical shorting that occurred. The fire ignited the internal plastic components and controls, which sent a fair amount of noxious and toxic smoke throughout the Quonset hut.

We killed the fire quickly with a CO_2 extinguisher and flipping the circuit breaker upon our arrival. But then we were faced with helping the medical staff move the soldier-patients to other nearby hospital units, away from the lingering smoke conditions, which was quite acrid overall.

Unfortunately we did not have any type of smoke removal fans in our arsenal of firefighting tools and hardware. We set up a couple of the floor fans to help assist in pushing out the smoke.

Most of these unfortunate soldiers were bed-ridden due to severe war injuries. Many were kept alive on various machines of critical life-support, and awaiting transport to advanced medical facilities in Japan, Germany, or Hawaii. I was shocked to see this sad part of war.

After that first call there, I became painfully aware of how the war tore men's lives apart, and that most would never be normal again. These images are burned into my memory forever.

I can still smell the stinging odor of that EVAC medical facility's electrical fire, mixed with the liberated Freon gas of that era's AC units. All of this continues to revisit me in a haunting manner. I dreaded responses to the hospital units, as the tragedy of war was very visible here.

SMOKE EATERS

During our assignment to the fire department all of the firefighters were exposed to various products of combustion and chemicals in the normal course of our assigned duties. There were no Self-Contained Breathing Apparatus (SCBA) nor filter type masks for us to use.

I still have an original copy of a DA 5-1 Fire Report in my historical treasure chest and it's copied at the end of this writing for historical note. This document shows that SCBA were not listed nor a part of our firefighting hardware. Back then, we were commonly referred to as either "Firemen" or "Smoke-eaters". These were proud titles of the professional fireman back then.

The limited stories that were printed in the <u>STARS & STRIPES</u> armed forces newspaper always mentioned us as "Firemen" or "Smoke-eaters". The news staff would usually identify us as base firemen in the first couple of lines of the article. Then we would be called smoke-eaters in the second paragraph or later on in the write-up. The term "smoke-eater" is not mentioned today.

In fact, stateside newspaper accounts of that era called firemen "smoke-eaters" regularly. Our military counterparts used the same written compliment for their reporting requirements.

Of interesting note is the fact that the word "Firefighter" wasn't even listed in the dictionary during that timeframe. I still have my copy of the full edition of Webster's 1967 dictionary, and there is no such word as firefighter listed. We were still "old-school" firemen!

Thus even in a war zone, the term "Smoke-eaters" was commonly used when our MOS and profession came to mind, especially when the news media covered our stories and actions.

I would like to also mention that women firefighters were not even in the equation here. Women were in the military at that time on duty at Long Binh, but they were always limited to their respective MOS, and assigned to medical, supply, office, or various support functions. Unless we had a response to where they were assigned, we did not see very many of them out and about.

THE BURNING ASSIGNMENTS

A most unusual duty was assigned to us by Army Command. They figured that since we were knowledgeable about fire behavior, suppression and control, then it would be ideal to also make us "firemen" in another aspect of our overall mission. We were to make fire!

We were soon trained on the operation and maintenance of the Army's flame-throwing gear and equipment. Making napalm was part of the program too. We became experts here, and MoGas and Ivory soap flakes permanently entered our fire department inventory and supply rooms.

Eventually I thought of Ray Bradbury's 1950s novel "Fahrenheit 451" that centers around firemen using fire to destroy books and educational materials in a futuristic society.

Thus, with this hardware and expendable material becoming a part of our inventory, it's another story well within itself to share for this document. Our duties were never boring.

One of the regular key duties that we performed was the burning of any vegetation after Agent Orange was sprayed on it. The Post Engineers (46th ENG BN) would spray various growth areas of the Post perimeter, and usually within two weeks, the brush and vegetation would be dead.

Unfortunately it did not disappear, as the dead vegetation still remained as a cluster or an item of bulk, and the Viet Cong could use it as cover at nighttime to harass and attack different areas of Long Binh. Thus, it became our job to burn the brownish and dead mass of vegetation to ashes.

With Chief Petersen's direction and clever record of modifying equipment, we turned 150 pound dry chemical extinguisher tanks into napalm vessels. Large pressurized air tanks provided the muscle to push the jellied napalm out of the tanks into the flame-thrower nozzles. It worked, and it worked very well. Our deployment of Napalm made everything "burnt toast".

There were countless times that we took our firefighting tank and track out on various burning assignments. The track vehicle carried our Napalm flame throwing equipment and fuel cell.

We worked these units long and hard at times. Engine troubles abounded at times. Sometimes these two units together were pulled back to our central station (Station 1) by a large Army Track Retriever after a completed burning mission.

Many times we were working downwind of the burning vegetation, and directly inhaling the smoke. We usually could not avoid the smoke drifting towards us, as certain strips of the Post's perimeter was saturated with land mines and the fencing of barbed wire. A "no man's land" for sure! Thus, being downwind of this burning activity was a nasty and unforgiving part of the job.

What we were never told about these burning missions was that the hazardous nature of all herbicides being used in Vietnam extensively could contribute to negative chronic health conditions. The baseline story here is that laboratory tests confirm that cancer can result from prolonged exposure to the inhalation and/or direct contact of these various chemicals.

THE AGENT ORANGE CONNECTION

The chemical, known as Agent Orange, was a killer herbicide. This product came in and was stored in fifty-five gallon metal drums. It was easily identified by a painted orange stripe around the center of its container. (Agents Blue, White and Green also existed and sported a painted stripe.)

Although a number of herbicides were used in Vietnam to help defoliate the jungles that enemy troops used for cover, Agent Orange was that which was used most extensively. It contained Dioxin, and that chemical element is what is persisting, and causing widespread affliction.

It was most effective in killing any vegetation, but it has caused vexatious cancer to anyone who came in direct contact with it, or was even in a nearby area. Too many military personnel and veterans are either now dead, or troubled by a wide variety of health and wellness issues, in addition to the ugly carcinogen oppressive aftermath.

Stomach sickness, vomiting, dizziness, shortness of breath, and dehydration followed us after most burning missions. Some of us got sick to our stomachs when we returned to the firehouse, and threw up, usually suffering severe headaches and dizziness during this timeframe.

What we were breathing was suspended particles of Agent Orange contained within the smoke cloud, plus all of the now very well-known and understood hidden poisons of the combustion process.

Sometimes we could sleep it off in our assigned bunks, and if it was too severe, then we self-administered oxygen to ourselves from the Inhalator that was carried in our rescue vehicle.

Nobody went on Sick Call. All of this was expected as being a "fireman" or a "smoke-eater" in our normal course of duties.

Today I have only approximately 39% of my Alveoli in my lungs left from the war chemical inhalation exposures. These assorted airborne exposures have resulted in the loss of my normal breathing capacity. There are times when I suffer severe shortness of breath, and must completely stop whatever I am doing, and quickly administer oxygen to myself.

I never thought that the unknown hazards of fighting fire and being exposed to negative airborne particulate matter would haunt me after fifty years.

The VA has recognized additional war related injuries and is now treating veterans for these health issues.

Congress has also passed new legislation in 2022 regarding burn pits and other toxic exposure coverage through the PACT act.

I have now joined the ranks of the Disabled American Veteran.

NO SCBA AND THE AFTERMATH

If one looks at and studies the various copies of articles and photographs of Army fire apparatus of that period, one would find out that there were no SCBA carried on any of the apparatus.

During this period of time in the fire service, such gear (if available) was carried on the outside of the apparatus for quick deployment, as it was practiced in countless American cities' fire departments. The Army was still behind the times then, at least in a war zone.

I truly believe that if we had SCBA back then, neither I nor the 51M's assigned would not have had the inhalation exposure to the various smoke conditions, unburned products of combustion, and war chemicals. Self-Contained Breathing Apparatus would have protected us.

There was one severe fire that involved PenePrime (road sealer). When PenePrime burned, it took on the dual properties of gasoline and diesel fuel. It became a scorching hot gasoline-like blaze with a heavy sustained fire load like diesel fuel, yielding an immense production of smoke.

A large number of 55 gallon drums caught fire in a laydown yard, and burned intensely for several hours. We were all downwind of the storage yard, since barbed wire fencing and land mines limited our firefighting efforts to come around the backside of the fire to fight it.

Near the end of that blaze, I ended up going to one of the Medevac treatment units for oxygen therapy and an IV infusion. I was extremely sick with smoke inhalation from that particular fire, and I was also severely dehydrated. The medics put dual IV's into me, as I was in trouble.

There was no rehab or rest period back then. One worked until you dropped at the scene of any fire or emergency. On long assignments, we would sleep on top of the hose beds, even in broad daylight, as we were that fatigued. We just covered our eyes with our soft caps.

One of the confusing parts of all of this, was that whenever a soldier-firefighter went to a medical facility for emergency care and treatment, we were listed and logged in as a PA&E employee, rather than that as an active duty member. Our medical records are lost forever.

It probably had to do with accountability issues since the Vietnamese civilian firefighters were on strike against PA&E across the country, and someone wanted to track the costs of having Army soldiers perform these duties with their related operational costs in contractor manner.

Overall, we were well treated at the medical facilities. It was usually a surprise to the medical staff that there were GI firefighters on the installation. No one gave us a second thought to our existence, nor even the rare MOS status, unless they had a fire and we showed up.

OUR TURNOUT CLOTHING

Our military issued firefighting turnout clothing was not much different than what the vast majority of American firefighters wore every day. It was an ensemble of three pieces of gear.

A composite plastic helmet, a canvas coat with four metal enclosure snaps and D-rings, and rubber ¾ pullup boots composed the standard issue. The helmets were black, the coat was olive drab, and the rubber boots were black with a small white rubber trim. There were no gloves issued for hand and finger protection.

The coat did not have a full interior liner. It was a vest type of liner. This wool fabric vest style liner did nothing to protect your arms from feeling the close encounter of heat conducting itself towards your skin during any hot atmosphere of firefighting. Burns were a commonplace injury for all of us during our duty time as firefighters. Leather trim adorned the cuffs and lower pockets for a reinforcement against the wear and tear points of the canvas coat.

Surprisingly the coat did have some narrow light reflective strips of the Scotchlite trim that was gaining widespread acceptance in the American fire service. That was pretty progressive for its time, as most turnout coats were always constructed in black canvas or rubber, with no trim or safety features. The coat has survived, and is in my collection of memorabilia.

There were no protective gloves issued. We hunted around the supply points for what they had, and there was nothing of value. We did find some painter's gloves, but they broke apart as soon as we used them at a call that involved rough handling conditions.

Since we had no outlet for hand protection, several of us wrote home, and got our families to send us some leather palm gloves from the States.

The brand "White Mule" were the best. They were a gauntlet style of glove, being well made and durable. It's interesting to note that the New York City firemen used and preferred these back then. We felt good that we were using what the "Big Apple" firefighters had.

When I took my R&R in Hawaii, I came back with about a dozen pair to have around, since we would tear them up sometimes on hard work service calls and needed a quick replacement.

The helmets were a lightweight fiberglass type of material. They were all issued in the color of black. There were no other markings on the helmets except for an "FD" on the front panel.

The PA&E chiefs took it upon themselves to personally order two white MSA hardhats for their headgear. These hardhats were made to have a fire department style leather frontpiece on the cap's panel for fireground identification.

I did the same and ordered an MSA traditional helmet in red, with a white frontpiece. It included the very first style of MSA's attempt at eye protection, which was a flip-down clear lens. It was not that much defense, but it offered some relief from airborne debris. (I still have my helmet.)

The boots were all rubber with an interior felt liner. These did not have steel safety toes, nor steel sole safety plates to protect against stepping on a nail. The invention of advanced impact and crush protection for firefighter footwear was still being developed in the states.

These boots were of what was known as the ¾ style. They were designed to be partially folded, and then pulled up to cover your thighs for additional protection. They offered poor protection against radiant heat, and once the boots got hot, they continued to be a great source of discomfort to you until you removed them.

These standard firefighter boots were suitable for encountering water situations and keeping your feet dry at best. They were ideal if we worked an off-road vehicle accident and one stepped off into a ditch with water, as there were snakes around. Fortunately we did have some protection against these unwanted creatures with this style of thigh-high boots.

It's important to mention that our boots were usually placed on the apparatus running boards and tailboards in between runs, and not on the floor. Seems like the small firehouse "guest" rodents and mice would enjoy crawling into them at times, and we preferred not to have any unnecessary surprises during our gearing up for responses.

"SILVERS" AND THE ASBESTOS EXPOSURE

One must first understand that our crash-rescue firefighting turnout clothing was asbestos lined. The silver reflective outer surface was bonded to a layer of asbestos, and then a lightweight rayon fabric vest covered that layer of clothing.

My exposure to using and wearing asbestos lined firefighter turnout clothing when on active duty in Vietnam obviously and directly contributed to my current state of asbestosis and emphysema.

Now my most recent medical examination has resulted in my breathing status being changed from emphysema to COPD. Asbestos is presently lying dormant in my lungs.

As a result of all of this occurring in the performance of our duties, I have only 40% of my lung capacity, due to the results of a combination of the toxic mix of burning vapors of Agent Orange, suspended particles of asbestos, and general smoke inhalation.

Approximately 60% of my Alveoli have been destroyed due to the chemical tissue attack of Agent Orange, mixed in with the toxic suspended smoke poisons. The Alveoli are permanently eliminated and will never grow back. Extensive VA and personal medical testing has confirmed all of this. I am living and breathing on less than the equivalent of one lung!

I was exposed regularly to asbestos throughout 1970 and 1971 whenever my fire company was suited up in our Crash-Fire-Rescue (CFR) personal protective equipment (PPE). We could have been on airfield standby at either of the two EVAC base hospitals, standing by at the main helipad of the USARV headquarters for incoming or departure missions of high-ranking leadership, responding to actual aircraft (fixed wing and rotary) fires and crashes, and POL types of fires during refueling mishaps.

It would not be uncommon to have donned this asbestos lined PPE on an average of three or four times during a twenty-four hour tour of duty.

One interesting part of this standby duty for VIP aircraft was seeing and greeting (in person) Generals Westmoreland and Abrams on an almost daily basis.

The generals flew via rotary wing aircraft, into Long Binh several times a week from Saigon to conduct and direct military operations at the USARV headquarters. And of course, all of the firefighters greeted their inbound and outbound flights in our asbestos lined "Silvers".

My connection with General Westmoreland led to two other unique stories in my life and career as a firefighter and musician. So that will come later.

The asbestos lined PPE that we wore was composed of an outer layer of an aluminized "Silver" surface to aid in the reflection of bright flames and radiant heat. This layer of protection was adhered to a backing of asbestos.

A lightweight snap-in nylon/rayon fabric liner was what covered the asbestos-lined outer shell. It was not airtight nor seamed in any way. The thought of this nylon/rayon fabric liner was to have provided a "dead air" pocket and layer to further assist in our personal protection.

Every time we donned or removed our PPE there would be flecks of asbestos liberated into our immediate atmosphere. These asbestos particles could be easily seen in the bright sunlight atmosphere of daily life in Vietnam.

The crash hood ensemble was also constructed this way. When we placed the fully encapsulating hood over our heads, we would be breathing these random asbestos particles.

Even our gauntlet style of turnout gloves were "Silvers" lined with asbestos. They had leather palms and the interior was a thin cloth like fabric for a liner. If one got a tear in this fabric, then one could easily see the asbestos lining.

You were usually sweating anytime you wore the crash PPE, so a moisture condition on your hands would act like glue, and the asbestos flecks would be visible upon one's skin.

It should be noted that SCBA was not part of the "Silvers" turnout gear.

It should also be noted that the design of these hoods would not have permitted the use of SCBA, even if SCBA was available.

In today's society of litigation, there are an abundant amount of lawyers whose entire practice focuses on the aftermath of workers being exposed to asbestos. The documentation is vast!

BADGES AND IDENTIFICATION

Of course we had GI "Dog Tags" stamped with our essential military information. These came about as soon as one was inducted and in the early stages of military processing. Our Dog Tags were a part of our lives as soldiers. We never took them off.

But with our duty in the fire department, we were also issued a standard Army Firefighter badge.

Nothing fancy, just a traditional silver finish crest badge with a firefighter "Scramble" in the center seal. No other inscription nor detail.

The top panel, where rank would be inscribed, was blank. The second panel from the top was worded "U.S. Army", and the next panel had "Fire Department" engraved. The lowest brief panel had "FD".

Several of us wanted a more traditional badge, with our rank on it, especially for a keepsake. In our discussion we felt and all agreed to have our initials and last name inscribed on the top panel. That way, if something happened to us, the badge would hopefully survive and our names would give us our identity.

So I wrote to the Braxmar Badge Company in New York City for assistance who were very prompt and most interested in helping us.

They were the premier badge producer in the United States at that time. So we knew that we were going to receive a very professional product.

Our badges arrived with our initials and last names inscribed on the top panel. They sported our corresponding rank on the center seal. I had two upright trumpets, the driver/operators had an image of an antique engine, and the bulk of the firefighters had a nice looking scramble.

The second panel had our rank/title and the third panel just below the center seal had "Fire Department". The small brief panel had "VN" inscribed. It stood for Vietnam, naturally.

Since we paid for these out of our own pockets, they were ours to keep and become a memento of our time served in Vietnam as military firefighters. To say the least, we were all very proud of our badges!

GENERAL FIREFIGHTING AND RESPONSES

During my time in Vietnam, I was exposed to many war chemicals including smoke, gas, and vapor conditions because of the vast warehouse district that we protected on Long Binh. Of course, there were many unknown toxins that filled our atmosphere whenever these chemicals and materials were severely burning. The aftermath of chronic health issues was completely unknown to us. Like I will continue to say throughout this writing, "it's just another fire".

We fought fires that involved PenePrime (road sealer), POL storage tank fires, POL pipeline flange and valve fires, insecticide and pesticide chemical fires, herbicide chemical fires, rodenticide chemical fires, various storage buildings that stored unknown commodities, warehouses that stored dry food supplies, a large warehouse fire that contained photographic supplies for nighttime aerial photography of suspected enemy movements, motor pool fires, vehicle fires, a large tire stockpile fire, shipboard and marine vessel fires that involved confined spaces and the holds of these ships, ocean-going barge fires, electrical fires involving air handling units, transformers, wiring, and underground communications centers, conventional weapon stockpiles that involved munitions and ammunition, barracks, mess halls, barber shops, wooden latrines, prison (LBJ) riot fires, grass and brush, and the list could go on and on.

Rescue runs, nuisance calls, and a plethora of other service requests kept us on a busy timetable.

Of course, our burning missions were also a part of our daily assignments. There wasn't any hard schedule for this work, as we were usually ordered to perform these actions within a given timeframe, after Command determined that such outlying vegetation was cover for the VC.

SAIGON FIRE BRIGADE

One of the first off base trips that I took with Chief Petersen found us going to the Saigon Fire Brigade. I really looked forward to visiting this major city's fire department, despite the war atmosphere, and could hardly contain my excitement to visit a metropolitan organization.

But first a little history about a major city's fire department influence on me. During my youth I enjoyed several visits to the Chicago Fire Department, and always found something new and interesting when I went. This Chicago connection was directly related to both Aunts being Catholic Nuns. My Dad took me to visit his sisters in Chicago several times, as they were Nuns of the Order of Saint Francis and were assigned to the Southside Catholic Diocese.

Through the planning of both Sisters, I was fortunate enough to visit several of Chicago's busiest firehouses in the toughest neighborhoods. In this timeframe of my youth I learned a lot about big city firefighting and unique apparatus. Thus, I felt somewhat prepared for this trip to Saigon Brigade. It turned out to be another eye opening experience in my young career as a firefighter.

As we entered the center of the City of Saigon, Chief Petersen pointed out a tall tower in the near distance. It was the location of the Fire Brigade, and it was the Brigade's watchtower that guided us in. We were soon coming to the main entrance and awaiting a security check and pass.

Once inside, we were greeted by a senior Brigade officer who spoke fluent English, and soon I was taken on a tour of the entire facility.

First of all, this was the sole fire station for all of Saigon. It was built like Fort Apache with very thick masonry walls that were quite high surrounding the entire installation. Approximately two hundred and forty firemen, with their families, lived in the quarters of the Brigade's compound.

Their apparatus and shops were all in close quarters with each other.

The watchtower was twenty stories tall and was manned 24/7/365. Of course, I had to get to the top of it and see the view of the City of Saigon for myself.

There was no elevator. Just an outside staircase that took several minutes of sustained leg work to ascend. One needed a well-conditioned heart and body to contribute to the overall success of this challenging climb.

The tower watchman would walk the exterior circular platform and occasionally bring a pair of binoculars to his eyes, and then concentrate on a particular siting. He explained to us that he would view anything he noticed which appeared to be an irregular part of the landscape.

An unusual cloud of smoke on the horizon during daylight hours gave rise that something was burning and required a prompt investigation. The location was pinpointed much like a forest fire tower notes landmarks and topography. Then apparatus would be dispatched to its estimated location.

A strange reddish glow at nighttime brought a similar response. Again, the tower's watchmen knew their city, and if something was amiss, then an alarm was rung for a unit to check on the situation.

Although Saigon was the largest metropolitan city of southern Vietnam, and quite modernized for its size, it still had its shortcomings regarding the reporting of emergency incidents. Thus, the watchtower was critical for overall fire protection.

The reporting of fires and emergency calls was accomplished by dialing "999", or by someone coming in directly in person to the fire brigade to request assistance. The "999" hotline number was originally established by the British telephone service exchange for emergency services dispatching within their country.

When the British were in Vietnam after World War II, they established this number for the City of Saigon, and it has served as the standard within the United Kingdom for numerous decades.

During my tour I noticed several makes of fire apparatus from across the globe in the fire truck stalls. I almost felt as if I were in a fire museum and enjoying a large selection of fire engines.

There were engines on the roster from France, Great Britain, Japan, Germany, and the United States. It gave credence that many countries helped Vietnam for many years after WW II to fight communism. Thus each country's fire apparatus became part of the professional landscape too.

When I got to the fire hose repair shop, I could not believe my eyes. There was a brigade technician working on a section of six inch diameter fire hose. I never knew that fire hose could be so large. After all, in the states we sported two and one-half inches as our "big' water supply hose. Some major cities sported three and a half inch hose for fireboat interface and support.

I went on to learn that large diameter hose (LDH) was utilized in most of the European countries, and that the couplings were of a 'sexless" design. This coupling was called a Storz, and it used a principle of a series of lug nuts to interlock with each other, thereby creating a watertight seal between the hose couplings. This meant that one could link up hose lines without regard to a proper combination of male and female thread fittings. It made things quick and simple.

The Saigon Fire Brigade had two large French pumpers that had large diameter hose inlets and outputs at the rear of each rig for major fires. This is where the LDH was attached, and for serious fires within the city or at the docks, this was the answer for moving large volumes of firefighting water.

The Saigon Brigade Fire Officer who gave me the tour explained that one of the French built LDH engines could easily supply two or three standard engines pumping at a serious fire.

These large rigs would usually draft water from the shoreline or one of the many water canals that ran throughout the City of Saigon. Their LDH could be run out for several thousand feet and move water in huge amounts. It would be almost two decades before the United States Fire Service started adopting this innovative and progressive method for moving water.

DOWNED AIRCRAFT CHALLENGES

When we went off the installation, it was always for a very serious call. In most cases it was for downed aircraft. We never knew what would greet us upon our arrival. We had to be extra keen of the environment, as the VC might be in waiting for us, since they could easily see a troubled aircraft coming down. We were always prepared for a different type of "firefight". Fight your way in, and fight your way out were the realities.

Many of these runs were truly long distance. We could go twenty or thirty miles to reach the crash site. Sometimes the aircraft landed safely, and things worked out well for everyone.

The Hueys could actually freefall to the ground, under certain conditions of no power, if the rotor blades continued revolving. A lot depended upon their overall mechanism not being damaged or impaired. It would be a "hard" landing for the troops, but survivable.

Then there were those incidents that hard-landed with injuries, sometimes fatalities, and maybe a fire. Extricating the injured away and out of the aircraft was paramount and immediate duty, especially if we had a fire situation, or an unstable fuselage or engine. This included the DOA's.

If we felt that related equipment failure could compromise anything else, then we took further action. Ensuring that the batteries were secure was always a necessary action. Ultimately we turned our attention to other required tasks that were prevalent at the scene.

There were times when the helicopter's main rotors were still turning under power. We all were very apprehensive about our approach to any troubled aircraft, because if I remember correctly, the Huey's main rotor blades were designed to revolve at 374 rpm under full power to make the craft go airborne. And that's a serious force of energy to encounter if things went wrong.

At least one driver/operator would be the lookout for any unfriendlies. He usually climbed to the top of the rig into an area that we called the "crow's nest", which was just above the pump panel.

That Soldier-Firefighter kept his eyes on a constant 360 degree scan, and with his peripheral vision he watched our backs. His full automatic M-14 was always at the ready.

Vietnam had bodies of water everywhere, and plenty of small streams, not to mention the abundant rice paddies. Sometimes our damaged and shot-up aircraft landed into these wet areas.

Obviously we could not drive our apparatus to these locations. Despite the nature of the 530-B fire engine that could supposedly "go everywhere", there were distinct limitations.

Thus we carried what equipment we needed upon our backs or over our heads literally to these crash points. It was not uncommon for us to hand-jack our twenty pound rated dry chemical cartridge extinguishers (which actually weighed close to forty-five pounds) a long distance. These alone weighed you down and wore you out, if you went any serious distance.

Medical first aid cases, litters, a resuscitator, the backpack cutting torch, and the metal pry bars and saws which were our extrication tools of the day, were also carried by sheer muscle. As I mentioned before, sometimes we could only carry these items over our heads, as the bodies of water were too deep. In fact, I can remember a couple of times when the water was chest high.

Vietnam was actually a very "wet" country. The Hollywood movies always showed the ever present and infamous rice paddies, but there were numerous small bodies of water everywhere. Thus, the jungle grew green and dense from all of the moisture, well hiding the enemy.

Whenever we had to cross into various bodies of water, we always did it in our "jungle" boots and fatigues. They worked out well for traveling to the sites. Our traditional turnout clothing really wasn't suitable for this. Plus the fact that this footwear gave us some secure footing that we did not seem to get from our traditional ¾ rubber boots. We usually swapped our steel "pots" for our firefighter helmets. They were lighter and we wanted that American style firefighter image to be projected and seen.

And there were times when some of us would trip on an object or something that we could not see below the surface of the cloudy water and fall down. It could be a ground-hugging vine, a clump of low level vegetation, or a piece of abandoned junk. The heavy pieces of gear that we were carrying would usually strike us on our bodies somewhere, and we suffered some type of impact injury. Again, no one complained or went on sick call; it was just another part of the job.

Usually I started shouting a standard phrase when we were getting close to the aircraft. I would yell as best as I could when carrying equipment, and used the words "American Soldier Firefighters from Long Binh. We're coming to help you. Stay calm. We're American Soldier Firefighters coming to help you". Of course, I kept repeating this, and the firemen also joined in with me to reinforce this message of arrival and rescue.

Sometimes if we felt and knew that the site was secure, then the driver/operator would blow a short blast on the siren. This let the downed aircraft personnel know that American help was nearby. I really don't know if this signal gave any comfort to the injured troops that the good guys have arrived. I hope that it offered some measure of assistance and security.

To the best of my knowledge during that timeframe, only American and Canadian emergency apparatus used electrical-driven mechanical sirens for an audio warning device. The Europeans used a dual-tone horn system of an alternating hi-low series of harmonic notes. Thus, the distinction between all of us. Maybe blowing the siren did something positive upon our arrival.

What always bothered all of us, and certainly strengthened our resolve in what we did as Army Soldiers, was that the NVA and VC shot at Medevac choppers. There was little respect for the articles of the Geneva Convention from these low-life communists.

In looking back, I can see that this was a prelude to what we all are facing in today's negative wave and environment of terrorism. I consider this to be the acts of cowards.

WATER, WATER, AND LEECHES

There was one nasty element to all of this, and that came from the ever present leeches. They would attach themselves to our forearms, and sometimes our facial areas, ears and necks, as we transgressed watery areas.

We dressed in our fatigues with rolled up sleeves in that tropical climate. We did not wear a full sleeve cover like today's troops do. Thus we had more skin area exposed. And we did not wear our turnouts when we were rushing across the ground to downed aircraft. Full gear would have actually impeded our work. Our battle fatigues were ideal for these missions.

After all, we were carrying heavy hardware and gear, and usually did not notice the leeches being on us until we stopped, unless one became attached to a facial area.

Then when we could have a pause in our work, we would get out our lighters and matchsticks to burn them off of us. Sometimes we needed each other's help to burn them off of the back of our necks.

The leeches could not be picked off in a traditional manner, like other pests. Their bodies were soft and there was no sizable bone structure, thus there wasn't any way to get a grip on their bodies.

The leeches actually "hooked" into our exposed skin areas. One could feel them the moment that they attacked us, and you could see their bodies swell, as they started to suck up our blood. They were downright scary when you looked at them enjoying themselves on your blood.

You could not pull them off, as it would be like trying to grab Jello. Plus the fact that they could cause a serious tear of your skin if you could grip them, as they were anchored into your skin much like a fish-hook could do to you.

As I mentioned earlier, it was not uncommon for us to wade into very deep bodies of water to reach the downed aircraft. Some of the times we were waist deep in water, and on a few occasions, we had water chest high. The leeches had a very annoying and bloody field day on us during these missions.

I still have regular nocturnal disturbances from my encounters with the leeches. I hardly ever sleep a full night without being awaken with a terrible skin condition that feels like I am being bitten all over my facial areas, neck, and forearms. I am sure that it's a PTSD condition.

Medical treatments and various medications have not helped. I struggle with this consistently.

As soon as we returned to our stations, we would shower and quickly change into dry boots and clothing, as the always wet bodies of ground water that we encountered hid various strains of bacteria. We regularly placed our wet fatigues and footwear out to dry in the hot sun.

Within a short period of time, we all suffered from a "jungle rot" between our toes and soles of our feet. We went to the medics, but nothing they issued to us worked to kill the fungus. Just another souvenir of the war as we said.

THE UNSAFE PRACTICES OF LIVE ORDNANCE FIREFIGHTING

Some of our work involved extremely unsound and unsafe practices, which is now strongly forbidden in today's firefighting world. In looking back, I will have to say that we were lucky.

The first item of business was that we fought Class 1 ammunition fires. Ordnance and munitions of any commodity was of precious value to the overall war effort. Without ammunition, all fighting, either offensive or defensive, simply stops.

Fighting any fire that involved live ammo is a Russian roulette venture. There is no sound data available that can advise one of when and how any amount of ammunition will behave when exposed to fire and extreme heat conditions. It could go off within any timeframe without any advance warning. And going high-order will probably result in death and/or serious injury to those nearby.

Military ordnance and munitions, once becoming unstable under the heat and exposure to a fire, will explode or become an "unguided" missile for a considerable distance.

Most of the ammunition fires involved the wooden shipment cases. That is how all ammo was stored and transported during the war. Ordnance was stored and carried within these wooden crates and containers, and wooden pallets were the standard platforms for almost everything we had.

Rocket attacks were usually what caused the fires to occur. Even a homemade rocket from the VC could easily ignite the bone dry wooden cases, and a handsome fire quickly presented itself.

We used straight streams of water upon burning wooden shipment crates from a distance, and also sought refuge behind anything that we thought would shield us. It was plain risky, and downright dangerous.

But this is what we did in a war zone as firefighters, and never really gave it a second thought in that young stage of our lives. It was just "another" fire.

There is one incident that will forever be with me, and how luck was on our side. There was a rocket attack against the ammo dump one evening, and a working fire was underway. A call was received from the ammo dump Officer of the Day to "double-time it to the ammo dump" as a serious fire was burning out of control. Thus, my driver/operator from Kentucky and I responded with the Tank to assist the small detail of Ordnance firefighters.

At this timeframe of the war, all ammunition fires were fought directly. This included ammo dumps, armed aircraft, supply trains, and other munitions carrying vehicles and apparatus. The thinking back then was to save the valuable ordnance, despite the severe life hazard to any of the firemen fighting the flames. One never knew when the ordnance would "cook-off" and kill those close at hand. Class 1 firefighting was simply a part of our duty.

This one scary situation did occur during this call from the rocket attack that resulted in a severe ammo fire. We were maneuvering the Tank around the burning wooden pallets and doing a pretty good job of knocking down the fires. Then all of a sudden, a single 105mm round "cooked off" and penetrated the left wall of the tank next to the driver's seat.

The Tank rocked violently when the round struck us. I thought that my driver/operator hit something, or that there was a deep pocket in the earth that upset the travel of the Tank.

After the 105 hit us, the travel of the Tank was immediately stopped, and I shut off the water flow from the nozzle. We paused and looked at each other in a confused manner. I asked the driver/operator what happened. He was a white as a ghost, and said to come and look inside his cabin space.

I went from my hatch position, and scooted over to the doorway of his driver compartment and saw the 105 round in the wall. I was in disbelief upon what I saw, and we were both using some pretty strong language as a result of the very visible shock of this encounter.

By a stroke of good luck, and an obvious blessing from above, it was a dud and did not detonate, despite knocking its tip through the three inch aluminum wall of the APC Tank.

The tip of the round was approximately three inches away from striking the driver/operator. Of course, our firefighters' nerves were never the same after that. And I still feel that first-hand today!

Many years later I located a model maker to work with me on the construction of a large scale model of the Tank. It is built in the approximate scale of 1/16th, and it authentically shows the hole of the 105 round's penetration.

During my time at Fort Polk, it was proudly displayed on the middle of the conference table in my office. It was always a topic of conversation to first-time visitors who came to my office. And it certainly served as a reminder of how lucky I was to have come home.

APPARATUS POSITIONS AND RESPONSE

The long-standing practice of riding the tailboard of the 530-B fire engines was an accepted part of the job. There were usually two to three firefighters on the back of each engine when responding.

If there were any VC or NVA sharpshooters around, it probably would have been easy for them to pick off the tailboard firemen, as they were fully exposed and unprotected.

One maintained a firm grip on the handrails until the engine arrived at the scene. There was no way for the two personnel in the cab to know if anything happened to the tailboard firefighters. If anyone fell off, neither the crew chief nor the driver/operator would know until we stopped.

Most of the 530-B's were governed to 45 mph, but some could get up to 55 mph. Imagine falling off at that speed. Serious injury, if not death, would be the result.

ROAD HAZARDS AND INJURIES ON RESPONSES

One would think that on an active duty military base, especially in a war zone with a dedicated MP detachment, that there would be good driving and safety on the roadways. Not so, as I will detail here.

One can only assume that bad driving habits are an inherent part of everyone's lives, and being a soldier in a theater of war does not correct the soldier's skills nor the situation about bad driving.

I truly believe that there were a number of our troops who were on drugs, legally prescribed or illegal, that were drivers of military equipment. They became involved in accidents, and this added to our overall responses and call volume both on and off base.

They caused damage and injuries, and added to the cost of doing business. Our own troops' actions were just as detrimental as the actions of our enemies could have inflicted.

Unfortunately a couple of us in the fire department were recipients of their impaired status. We were lucky that we did not get killed by their poor driving habits on the roadways of Long Binh.

An incident happened to me towards the end of my time in country, and it could have been real serious. I got lucky once again, to say the least.

Engine 3 was returning from an out of control burn pile fire, and we were on the home stretch coming back to the station just before dusk. I was the only GI on the apparatus, and the crew was composed of four Vietnamese contract firemen. This was because the war was truly being converted to a total South Vietnamese operation, and vetted civilians were taking our places, permitting us to go home.

I was driving the rig since none of them were trained on the fire apparatus. They were scheduled to have a program of instruction and operation with the driving course first, and then to pass the test to become a Driver/Operator for PA&E.

I was driving in my lane and all of a sudden a heavy 2-1/2 ton truck crossed the center of the road and was coming at me head-on! I quickly pulled way over to the shoulder of my side of the roadway, and this other truck just followed me.

The next thing that happened was that we narrowly missed each other, but both of our outside mirrors came into contact with each other. There was a sharp crack of noise upon the impact and glass went everywhere, especially inside the cab of the engine.

I stopped immediately and was in a state of disbelief. The other truck just kept on going down the road. I could not see it very well nor get the marking numbers, as my mirror was gone.

Then I felt a pain in my upper left arm, and felt my face getting wet. What I quickly discovered was that several pieces of glass mirror fragments became imbedded in my skin and facial areas.

There was a large piece that stabbed me in my upper left arm, and that was starting to smart. I jumped out of the cab, and ran to the other side of the rig and looked in the right hand side mirror to see what happened to me.

The Vietnamese firemen all gathered around me, and started to pick out the visible pieces of glass from my body and fatigues. They were talking in half Vietnamese and half English during this action. One of them went for the first aid kit, and he started getting some dressings out to treat me.

Upon pulling the shard out of my arm, I knew that the damage from this large piece of glass was a serious injury, and that I needed advanced medical assistance. And yes, I was bleeding across my face and left ear areas from the other impact areas of the glass shrapnel by now. Thus, I told them to get on the rig, and then I drove over to the 24th EVAC hospital.

At the 24th EVAC I got seen right away by the medical staff. They cleaned my wounds, applied dressings, and gave me a Tetanus shot. I was told to return there tomorrow for a follow up, and to ensure that no infection was taking hold.

We returned to the station, and I had to deal with a couple of weeks of keeping bandages on my wounds, until my skin healed. The upper arm wound hurt for several weeks. I knew then that any type of stabbing injury was a serious event.

After I calmed down at the station and had a Coke, I did walk over to the MP station across the road, and reported the incident. The MP NCO said that they'll try and see if they can find the truck. I never heard back from them. It's just war and another crazy incident in the overall mix of things.

Once again, none of this was recorded in my medical records. More lost history for both me and my service time in the Army in a theater of war.

The second event involved my beloved Driver/Operator from Kentucky and he was in the Tank when his incident happened!

The Tank was special called by me to a working fire on the POL pipeline outside Gate 9 one day.

I was already there with both engine companies and the water tender, but we needed the Tank to transverse the terrain. We simply would have had to dump both hose beds and hand-jack all of our 2-1/2" to get to the blazing couplings and spilled fuel. And then rolling up two thousand feet of hose would have made the job an unsafe mission as dusk was soon upon us. The Tank would have made the job a brief encounter.

As my Kentucky driver was coming through Gate 9, a small jeep darted in front of the Tank. He had to abruptly pull the drive handles back to dead stop in order for the Tank to keep from running over the jeep and killing its soldiers.

Unfortunately, this action caused the driver to hit the front rim of the hatch, and thereby his jaw came in contact with the hard metal circular ring. He had fractured his jaw in a high school football game, and thus he broke it again.

Time passed and I wondered "where the heck was the Tank?" After I asked myself that question an MP jeep came to the fire and advised me of the crazy news of the near-miss accident.

I told my driver of Engine 3 to go back with the MP and bring the Tank here since the Tank's driver was on his way to the 24th EVAC for treatment of his injuries.

Once the Tank arrived, the fire was quickly knocked down, and I then drove Engine 3 with its crew over to the 24th EVAC to check on the status of the driver.

Fortunately an MP jeep crew took the injured driver to the base hospital for medical care. And they stayed with him until our arrival.

He was stable, sore, and downright mad about the stupid jeep soldier. We never did figure out who the accident culprit was, otherwise he would have been a punching bag for the firemen somewhere down the line.

The driver spent the night at the 24th, and then we picked him up in the morning. He had some type of wire brace around his jawline to help things heal faster. I knew that he had to be uncomfortable.

He did not want to go on sick call and spend his time at some barracks recovering. Instead, he stayed at the fire station, doing odd jobs, like refilling fire extinguishers for the post, and assisting the RTO when things got busy in the radio room with communications.

We all were family and being away from each other was not in anyone's makeup as a firefighter.

In looking back I feel that we were lucky once again. War zones include the careless!

EYE AND VISION INJURIES

Minute debris provoked eye injuries to become somewhat commonplace. There wasn't anything available for us to have for eye protection. Firefighting goggles, or any type of eye or face shield, were not invented at that time.

After working in a smoky or ash filled atmosphere of a fire, one could easily have eye troubles resulting from the dirty environment.

Thus, it became standard practice for one to use a gentle stream of water from the booster line to assist in the flushing of one's eyes. If the booster tank's water was brackish or was empty, then one used canteen water to help clean your eyes.

There were times when some of us had to go to one of the EVAC hospitals for treatment. Our eyes actually got scratched, and the medics flushed our eyes several times to ensure that nothing remained on our eyes. They also issued eye drops with a numbing action to give us some relief.

I wish to mention here that since our helmets had none of this protection, it would also be commonplace for the firemen to reverse the position of their helmets against high levels of radiated heat. The long rear brim afforded some relief as a shield when we encountered such conditions of radiated heat from large open flames of the burning process.

DENTAL CARE OR LACK THERE OF

There was a dental clinic at Long Binh. But the care that one might expect was simply not present. The standard of care was lacking to say the least.

If one required a simple filling, then you might be in luck if there was material available for the work. Dental care just wasn't a high priority for the Army in a war zone.

I suffered a severe fall at a mess hall fire, and impacted my left facial area by the lower jaw. My skin was broken and I had a severe inner cheek cut. I bled pretty intensely for an hour or so, and then the bleeding started to slow down. A couple of more hours passed and then I could remove the heavy gauze pads from the inside of my mouth without additional hemorrhage.

Unfortunately for me, I suffered a crack to one of my molars during the fall and impact. In about two days, a fractured piece of the tooth fell out and as a result, I had a very jagged edge line on my molar. Thus, I went to the dental clinic for repair, or so I thought.

The dentist looked me over, and said that there was nothing he could do to repair or save my molar. He said that it had to come out to prevent any further complications.

In hindsight I should have just filed off the rough edges with a small file from the tool room and lived with it until I got home.

Next thing I knew was s small shot of Novocain coming my way, and after some serious pulling, the molar came out. The minute injection of Novocain did little to provide me some comfort, and after the bleeding stopped, I looked at my absent tooth area, and knew that this would not be good for me for the rest of my life.

I am glad that I had good teeth and did not encounter any other serious dental incidents while in country.

A CLOSE CALL IN THE AIR

This was a true war zone. Soldiers and civilians were getting killed and/or seriously injured every day in performance of their duties, or just simply living. I consider myself lucky to have come home, and I offer sincere thanks to my Eternal Chief that I am home safe and sound.

There are several events that shook me into the awareness of the fragile state of one's life. On one bright and sunny day, I went off base to inspect a FOB's firefighting equipment, which consisted of multiple large capacity wheeled dry chemical units and assorted hand-held extinguishers.

I rode a small helicopter to the site. It was the Bell unit that was affectionately called an "Egg-Beater". Normal Army nomenclature was the Kiowa.

During the trip in we started taking small arms ground fire. The warrant officer flying the Kiowa really knew his job, and how to evade such attacks. What happened next was a series of airborne evasions that I never knew was possible to conduct with any type of flying aircraft.

Fortunately at this time there were no "smart" bombs and missiles as weapons of war. All things entered into the equation of a weapon hitting its target. This included, and was not limited to, the aim of the weapon, unstable factors of the weapon's delivery power, windage, and just plain good luck. I suspect whatever came at us was a small rocket, possibly an RPG (Rocket Propelled Grenade) type or a homemade device.

The warrant officer pilot maneuvered the aircraft skillfully and yet abruptly to avoid being hit. He dropped altitude and evaded whatever was coming at us. It felt to me that the aircraft must have fallen a thousand feet within one second, and spun around in a circle with a severe gravitational force reaction.

Whatever airborne ordnance was coming our way fortunately did not strike the aircraft. It had to be close.

Thus the severe change in altitude caused my left ear drum to rupture, and then I immediately got sick to my stomach when we leveled off from the rotational condition. I ended up vomiting into my ball cap.

So I live with this "Beethoven" condition, which is a hearing loss in my left ear, and tinnitus.

The tinnitus can be very annoying at times. There is little one can do to relieve this affliction. One just has to accept the fact, adjust to it, and live with it.

As I continue to be an active musician today in church and several bands, I am thankful that additional damage did not occur. I am fortunate whereas I can still enjoy performing my music within the overall noise and sound environment of tinnitus.

THE ORPHANAGE

My next close call involved the Sisters of Charity Orphanage which was a few miles away in a rural type area from Long Binh. The Sisters took care of the war orphans, and it was a sizable institution, holding many children of all ages. It was a most remarkable undertaking within a war zone regarding what the Sisters accomplished with care for these young lives.

Since they received no immediate type of fire protection response from anyone, the PA&E fire chief made a decision to help place several fire extinguishers throughout the orphanage.

LBFD firefighters rebuilt a number of surplus CO_2 and dry chemical units into workable assets.

Thus, the Sisters were to have some 1st aid type of fire protection until we could get there or one of the nearby village fire brigades, which were all volunteer dependent.

Normally two of us went to deliver the extinguishers, but on this particular day I went solo. It turned out to be a bad idea. A number of suspected VC noticed me being at the orphanage. They came out of hiding, and started forming a "street gang" near the parked fire jeep.

I could feel the tension in the air when I noticed them outside on the roadway. I only had my turnouts with me, and no war gear. Just my fatigues, LBFD ball cap, and carrying my .45 caliber. I felt that my luck had run out, and figured that I was going to get captured or killed, and the end was coming.

Before I got into the jeep to make a run for it, one of the Sisters came out and directly confronted the VC members. She spoke sternly to them in Vietnamese, and they left me alone, despite their numbers not dispersing. I did my best in acting cool while getting into the jeep, and drove away in a normal fashion.

I found out later that what she told them was that the GI firemen were the only ones who helped the orphanage. She said that they received free fire extinguishers, and the Sisters needed that protection.

The Sister also went onto say that if any of them would hurt any of us, then the wrath of God would be upon them.

Plus, she reminded them that we were the good guys, the ones who would always come and help the village fire brigades. What the Sister said to them evidently worked, plus it was the truth.

From that time forward, the LBFD Cuu Hoa (Vietnamese for firemen) were respected by the VC, left alone, and never harassed or threatened directly when off base.

After all, many of the VC lived in the villages that we assisted, so their homes were protected by us. Despite the war differences, the VC wanted our protection of their homes and families.

IN THE DARK AND ALONE ON A RESPONSE

We received a call for a fire at our pipeline terminal one dark night around two in the morning. I can't remember all of the exact details, but A/C Cha told me to drive the foam tender that carried the protein foam, and to follow him.

Enroute to the response, he went through a construction zone, where the roadway was being rebuilt. He was driving the Deluge Jeep, and he motioned for me to take the same route of travel.

I opened the door and stood on the running board yelling that I felt it was too unsafe. I saw the struggle that the Jeep had when it transversed this patch of roadway, and felt that the foam tender would sink. He kept waving his hands and shouting back at me to follow him.

As soon as the tender got midway into the roadway, it sank into the soft roadbed, and I was immediately stuck. I then placed the transmission into low range and shifted to the lowest gear to drive all six wheels.

It did not work. All I did was cause the rig to sink in further when I applied power to the power train. A/C Cha then realized that I could do no more.

He said he would go on ahead to the fire and get back to me later. Cha also said he would call headquarters station to get a wrecker or tank retriever to come and pull me out, and for me to stay with the rig.

Unfortunately I did not have a radio mounted in this rig. Several pieces of our apparatus were not equipped with a two-way radio. This is where it got scary.

I was alone in this disabled vehicle, and in total darkness. There was no moon, and it was pitch black. I grabbed my weapons and ensured that they were in the ready mode for a firefight. I felt that I would be attacked, and that the end would be near real soon.

Long Binh was several miles behind me, and I had no immediate measure of security to pacify me. I figured that I was in one heck of a mess.

Fortunately I did have my hand lantern with me. In the dark night I could still see the southern-most watch tower of Long Binh as I looked back towards the base. I then thought that I might as well try and use my lantern to flash an SOS back that direction.

I pointed my lantern towards the watchtower and started flashing the Morse code towards the base. I kept it up for a good four or five minutes when I then saw an acknowledgement signal flash back at me. I knew that a scouting party would soon head my way.

Within a half hour or so, a small squad of soldiers showed up, and was I ever relieved. I immediately thanked them for coming, and advised them of what happened.

Their RTO called back to Long Binh and got a tank retriever to come. The squad set up a perimeter and waited with me until the retriever arrived.

The recovery went well and I got pulled back to the fire station without any further hiccups.

I must admit that this was a tense situation for me, without question!

POST 1'S PILLBOX

LBFD had our own "pillbox" for pulling night-time watches to assist in the guarding of our perimeter of the installation. It was given the number "Post 1", and rightfully so, since it was on the backside of Fire Station 1's lot. It also faced Highway 1.

On one night there was some movement in the distance, and the duty soldier-firefighters called for me to come in haste. Looking through our primitive infra-red scopes, we could see several "greenish" shapes in the distance. Soon we started seeing a lot of the green images.

I stepped outside the pillbox and sent up a white flare to illuminate the area. Once the flare went airborne, and started burning its bright light, we could clearly see a large number of VC coming our way. This was definitely a large group coming straight towards us.

I quickly popped a red flare into the sky above our location, which informed everyone around us and the headquarters staff watch, that we were encountering a hostile force.

Muzzle flashes were now seen across the highway, so I told the on duty pillbox crew to "open up" and fire at will. I was supposed to call on the field phone first and request permission to open fire if we became engaged. Staying alive was all I cared about at that moment.

I did call as weapons were being discharged, and loudly yelled into the phone that "Post 1 is under attack", and then I hung up and joined the firefight.

We basically shot at any image that appeared within our scopes. Filling the air with hot lead was what we accomplished during these encounters. We wanted to neutralize any enemy threat.

When daylight returned in the morning, we would scan the approximate area of movement to see if any visible signs of bodies were on the ground. We never did see anything, and felt that if we shot anyone, then these bodies were removed before darkness left the landscape.

Long story short, the attack was thwarted, and the VC quickly disappeared back into the night during the initial stages of that encounter.

We were not bothered anymore during the duration of our time there after that night. I figured that I was going to be in a heap of trouble with command after that event, since I did not follow the established protocol of calling headquarters on the field phone first before returning fire.

Being the NCOIC made me 100% responsible for any and all offensive or defensive actions. Fortunately I heard nothing that evening nor the next day from anyone in command.

After this encounter, I started paying closer attention across the installation to nighttime flare activations. Seems that many red flares were sent up in the sky on various evenings, giving one the impression that the VC had not stopped in their quest to do us all in.

Letting one's guard down could be fatal for one or all of us. It was serious business pulling guard duty in any of the installation's pillboxes at night.

The war was real and after this incident, it came to our front door.

I knew that smart decisions had to be made within a split second. It was truly better to err on the side of safety, and be prepared for action against a hostile force, large or small.

America's involvement in South Vietnam, to sustain democracy, was something that drove our enemy to fight us every step along the way. Even small attacks were their trademark for resistance, and the fall and retreat of Allied Forces was their endgame.

The communists were determined to remove us and our allies, and take over South Vietnam. I became immediately convinced that they would never let up in their quest to accomplish all of this.

THE WAREHOUSE DISTRICT AND A SABOTEUR'S ACT

On an extremely warm afternoon a saboteur struck the warehouse district. His mark of fire was one of the two large photographic supply warehouses. All of the fire phones started ringing at once, and LBFD firefighters were already suiting up, and began walking over to their rigs.

Our first call came from Station 4 in the warehouse compound. They advised that they were responding to a burning warehouse, and requested Station 1's assistance, as the rising smoke condition could be easily seen from their apparatus apron.

Upon Station One's arrival, we found one of the two warehouses already heavily involved in fire, and becoming a serious threat to its unburned partner. We did not want the blaze to communicate to the other warehouse, as we knew that this unburned warehouse contained high value war material. We truly knew that a long battle of firefighting was to begin.

These two warehouses stored massive quantities of photographic supplies for the support of the airborne surveillance mission which was conducted nightly over the suspected NVA and VC supply routes.

The flash powder drums started to erupt and go "high-order" which added to the magnitude of the fire. The metallic building was also starting to discolor as the fire grew in size. Parts of it were starting to fatigue and slope inwards, making it difficult for the hose streams to penetrate the fire.

Fortunately for us this warehouse district was protected by an underground looped water network that supported multiple fire hydrants. It was fed from a two million gallon reservoir with dual diesel driven fire pumps both rated at one thousand gallons per minute delivery.

We started laying out hose lines from the nearby hydrants, and soon the pavement was full of "spaghetti" for the forthcoming firefight.

PA&E Chief Petersen told all the pump operators to connect to the steamer connections with their hard suction for maximum water flow intake. The steamer connections were of the four and one-half inch NST standard. None of Long Binh's apparatus carried any soft suction in the steamer style. Just hard suction hose in ten foot lengths with 4-1/2" NST couplings.

Thus, this was the only manner in which to obtain each engine company's maximum fire pumping capacity of 500 GPM. And yes, it was time consuming and difficult to mate the very stiff hard suction hose to the hydrants.

Chief Petersen also told everyone to deploy two and one-half inch hand lines for the fire attack.

He also called Station One via the radio to have someone bring the Deluge Jeep to the scene. The on duty GI RTO brought the jeep as soon as he was relieved by the incoming local Vietnamese PA&E contractor department secretary. The heavy master stream appliance would be sorely needed here to help knock down the massive blaze.

It should be noted that at this timeline of the department's operation, the makeup of its firefighting members was being converted over to the PA&E contract workforce, and our fire crews were becoming a mixed sort of personnel. I believe that only four of us GIs were left. Just about everyone else went home at this timeframe.

Things were really going negative for us on this fire in the beginning. We focused the heavy hand lines on the second warehouse and kept that structure's exterior walls as cool as possible.

We also had two lines boring into the heart of the fire through the open main doorway. Of course, the fire received plenty of air to sustain its burning with the large open door.

There were about twenty firefighters total at the scene. Obviously, the Crash station personnel could not leave their duty station, as the constant flow of Medevacs would keep them busy.

We started bolstering our firefighting ranks with soldiers. They were glad to assist in handling and manning the heavy hose lines, and gave all of us some needed relief.

As the fire burned and I would give it the height of the blaze, I was helping a three member PA&E contract Vietnamese fire crew from Station 3 reposition their 2-1/2" hand line to move closer to the burning interior of the open doorway.

Then a flash powder drum, of the thirty gallon capacity, cooked off and exploded. The chemical powder went everywhere and lit up in an explosive manner. The sound was deafening and earth shaking. The lid of the drum went flying like a guided missile straight to me. I was in front of the Vietnamese firemen, and knew there was no time to move out of its travel path. I just stood my ground, acting as a human shield, hoping no one else would get hurt.

Before I knew it, the lid hit me in the chest, and body slapped me to the ground. There was no time to react, and I really couldn't, as I was also dragging the heavy hose line with the three Vietnamese firefighters when I took its impact. It all happened in a split second.

I was wearing one of the new Hypalon turnout coats at this fire. The newly developed turnout jacket came from Halprin Supply of Los Angeles. It was a very lightweight fabric and had a dull silver colored outer shell. Fortunately the coat offered a level of protection against the impact.

When I got up from the ground, I composed myself and went back to assisting the crews. I did not know that I suffered any injuries, although I knew that I took a hit of some sort.

The RTO immediately came over to me after witnessing the event, saw my injuries and told me that I needed to go one of the EVAC hospitals for medical attention.

At first I did not understand what he was talking about, then I looked at the front of the silver turnout coat, and found it to be a bright red. I was bleeding from my chin, jawline, forehead, and the skin area of my right eye. My right side of my chest and stomach area began to hurt also. I told the RTO that I will be alright, and walked away from him, going back to the fire line. After all, this was a major fire and fighting the fire was more of an immediate concern for me, than another injury which could be dealt with later on, after the fire was under control.

About twenty minutes passed by and Chief Petersen came over to me, and ordered me to go to one of the medical facilities. He said that he felt the fire was under control, and that I could be relieved. He said that my bleeding needed to be taken care of.

The RTO then drove me to one of the EVAC hospitals in the Chief's pickup. There I was started on dual IV's, as I lost a fair amount of blood, my vitals were very abnormal, and I received some serious lacerations. I guess I got to the EVAC at the right time, since I was becoming very dizzy and wanted to faint.

I nearly lost my right eye as a piece of shrapnel caught the corner of my skin, just before the eye socket. A small piece tore my upper left eyelid and left cheek. My chin was deeply cut and bleeding openly. There were several other puncture points on my face where small fragments of metal tore into my facial skin. And I have a small circular scar on my right side lower lateral chest wall. That area hurt and felt like I took a round. I can still see the faded scars to this day despite the passage of time, and my left lower lip scar is pronounced.

The EVAC medical team and staff were rock solid professionals. They were at a quiet moment of their duty time, and turned their full attention to the treatment of my injuries. I was kept there for several hours to ensure that I would be alright. Their medical work and concern for me was outstanding.

Upon my return to the station, Chief Petersen told me to go and get some rest in the bunkroom, and he said he'd check on me later. Fortunately for us, it was quiet around the station for almost two full days before calls started coming in. I slept until almost noontime the following day, as that fire and my related injuries wore me down.

This incident occurred approximately two weeks before I was to ETS. Thus, I came home with fresh war scars and stitches.

I am very lucky.

MEDALS, RECOGNITION, AND RECORDS

Since I remained steadfast on the fire ground for the warehouse fire, and ignored my own injuries, Chief Petersen put me in for a Purple Heart and the Bronze Star. He heard about what happened, and felt that I deserved some recognition. Even the Vietnamese firemen told him that I "stood in front to protect them and took the impact with great courage".

I came home with neither of these recognitions being awarded. I did inquire about them at the In/Out Processing Center in San Francisco as I was being mustered out. No paperwork was to be found in my records at that time. To date, I never received either medal.

Many years ago I did again check on the status of these submittals, but nothing can be found within the Army's records system. It was probably due to the mixed nature of the staffing of the fire department's personnel of soldiers and contractors, and the war ending for the United States.

Someone probably thought that all of Long Binh's firefighting personnel were contractors, and were not entitled to military awards, and the paperwork ended up in the circular file.

One other notable point to mention is the fact that the Combat Infantry Badge was not awarded to those who fought in support units. You had to be assigned to a combat unit. Medals were not easily handed out to many who deserved something for their tough times and encounters.

After the war ended for us, PA&E shrunk to a very small operation for contracting services. I found out that they still had a small office in Washington, D.C. Thus, I did contact them for their records on Long Binh, thereby hoping to find some of the PA&E chiefs and other personnel.

I was informed that no records exist for their involvement in the support of the war in Vietnam. Their office manager wasn't even born when I was in country, and she tried to find someone to assist me from that timeframe within their retired personnel section, but alas to no avail.

More lost history.

ANOTHER ROCKET – ANOTHER FIRE

One evening a rocket hit one of the Engineers' barracks. It didn't take long for the structure to become heavily involved in flame. After all, these were completely wooden buildings, with a projected life span of five years. Everything was built of wood except for the asphaltic shingles or metallic sheeting for the roofs.

The Engineers' compound was directly south of the main station, and as we mounted our apparatus, one could see a cherry red glow lighting up the sky. Our station faced due south, so everything was quite visible to us at the initial alarm and response.

Upon arrival, we pulled our pre-connect lines and started playing water upon the burning structure, as there were no trapped soldiers. Good luck happened for the quartered soldiers from that barracks, in that no one was hurt or killed from the impact of the rocket. The troops were fortunately at another area enjoying a movie.

We had to call for water tanker support, as this was a large two story barracks, which would require lots of water to suppress the heavy fire condition facing us. Soon we received a number of the five-thousand gallon potable water tanker units from across the installation, and we felt comfortable that we will have adequate water to suppress the fire.

We were well into the overall fire suppression when another rocket came into our area. It did not hit anything nor any personnel. Fortunately it impacted at a nearby open laydown strip of land, that was used for large vehicle storage. But it caused us to drop the hose lines, and rapidly head for the protection of our apparatus.

As soon we got to our rigs, we grabbed our steel helmets, flak-vests, and M-14s, and then all of us low-crawled under the 530-Bs, and stayed in that position until we felt no further incoming rockets would bother us.

The suppression of the fire became a secondary concern versus any future incoming rockets. Receiving protection from our trusted apparatus was paramount. After a few minutes passed, we crawled out from under the apparatus, and went back to fighting the fire at the barracks.

FIRE SCENE INVESTIGATIONS AND INCIDENTS

Not every fire was fully investigated as to what actually caused a fire. By making that statement I mean that some incidents were extremely obvious and warranted no extra attention. We simply made an appropriate comment, when we felt it was necessary, on the DA 5-1 Fire Report.

A point in case was any fire that did not grab some authority figure's attention. Grass and trash fires that were extinguished without any damage to military property were ignored in most cases.

Several fires that occurred in some of the barracks were usually attributed to careless smoking and soldiers doing stupid things. A common mistake was the overloading of wall outlets with numerous fans plugged in. Soldiers did things for personal comfort and relief from the heat.

One incident found about a dozen fans being fed off of one wall outlet. That event brought forth a combination of overheated components, causing the insulation properties of the plastic coated extension cord wiring to fail, short out, and result in a fire.

Several of these fires occurred during the evening time when soldiers were sleeping. Fire watches should have been maintained, but it was lax in many units. Everyone was tired and wanted their rest. Fire prevention was not taken seriously in some of the units.

Since these barracks were of the open bay two story design, they did not have any HVAC or single air conditioning units, nor ceiling fans to keep soldiers comfortable.

One was on their own to find relief from the heat when they were not on duty and resting. The Post Exchange sold hundreds of electric fans to everyone. So if common sense was not used for the extensive use of electrical equipment, then a fire could take place.

It should be noted that smoke detectors had not been invented yet. The single station solo zone battery powered smoke detector did not come on the market until late 1978.

Only an alert soldier performing fire watch duties could keep his brothers-in-arm safe at night.

He would be the first line of defense against any fire incident when everyone else was asleep.

The detail of his duty meant that he also had to diligently keep roaming the barracks during the nocturnal hours, and watch for any incipient stage of fire occurring.

Since the beginning of time we know that every living creature, except for a dog, loses their sense of smell when they slumber. A dog's nose works 24/7. It never sleeps. Dogs are and have been responsible for saving countless lives during the initial stages of fire throughout the years.

As a young fireman, I used to teach in my fire prevention classes to young school children that it was okay for the family dog to sleep with you, or in a hallway near the bedrooms, as they will alert you to any smoke condition or fire incident. (I learned this from Commissioner Quinn of the Chicago Fire Department, who wrote an article about this worthwhile lifesaving measure.)

Some of the other causes of fires were soldiers and contractor personnel doing ordinary work and not thinking safety first. Some fires were easily preventable, and common sense was absent.

We had one serious fire at the motor pool one morning. The soldier-mechanics worked twelve hour shifts on military vehicles, and shortly after the night crew went off duty, a fire occurred.

A 1-1/4 ton vehicle was in for carburetor replacement and some pass-along information got dropped from the evening shift to the oncoming personnel.

This vehicle had its hood down, and it looked like it was ready to go out in the yard, awaiting for its unit's personnel to pick it up. Unfortunately, the carburetor was sitting on the work bench. A mechanic went to start it, for the purpose of moving it to the yard, and a fire quickly ensued.

What happened here was that raw gas started squirting from the carburetor's fuel line under the hood, and the fuel became ignited by the spinning electric starter. The mechanic was both shocked and scared when this occurred, thus he quickly exited the vehicle in a state of panic.

Unfortunately he left the ignition switch on, and the electric fuel pump kept running, feeding the growing blaze. Essentially a running fuel fire was taking place, and this creates a tough situation for any firefighting crew to face and extinguish.

As we drove up we could see that a serious working fire was developing quickly, as there were now two other vehicles catching fire.

Part of our challenge here was that a slight slope of the floor was contributing to the running nature of the freely flowing Mogas, and it was burning very well and hot.

We quickly killed the fires on the two adjacent vehicles, and turned our attention to the original source. A blanket of foam was shot at the running spill fire, but it had no effect.

After raising the hood, a second foam line was applied to the open butt of the fuel line, but the flowing Mogas just kept burning. A risky situation and some raw courage then took place.

One of the firemen took a rag and a screwdriver, and approached the fuel line from its least offensive and burning side of the open flame. As pure fuel does not burn, only the vapors, he shoved the rag into the piping as a water spray curtain was applied. He therefore plugged the leak, and the fuel stopped flowing. The fire was promptly extinguished from that point.

That he was both lucky and brave was an understatement. Our plan of action was to keep our fire streams on the overall burning process, and await the total consumption of fuel for final extinguishment. His courageous work saved us a lot of time and effort.

Basically the causes of some of our fires were simply the result of soldiers being human, and our military society was no different than civilian society. We all make mistakes, and have to live with our results, and try to do better in the future. Thus, we have fires mixed up in our lives.

SMELLS AND RELATED AFFAIRS

I must mention smells. In particular, cooking smells that I strongly associate with troubled times and dangerous situations. To this day, I never visit an oriental restaurant nor enjoy fish or chicken. These particular odors of cooking can set my mind into the motion of returning back to a very nasty situation in Vietnam.

During a couple of our runs for assistance to the local fire brigades of small villages, I encountered seeing a strange collection of raw food items consumed by the local Vietnamese. Viewing items like fish heads and small hanging bodies of red meat, actually spooked me.

Fires and other ugly events were sometimes tied to the cooking odor of various foods and staples that were consumed by the local Vietnamese. A time and place is stamped in my mind forever.

I am haunted when I encounter these. I fully feel that I must be back in a war zone, and that my life is threatened. None of this has lessened for me during this passage of time.

I can only assume that this is a part of PTSD for me.

THE TUGBOAT FIRE AND A FATALITY

One of the most shocking incidents occurred when we were called for a tugboat fire near our POL docks. It was my first encounter with a burned body, and the never forgiving smell of burnt flesh.

The smell and odor of burning human flesh is distinctive, and one never forgets its impact.

This was a fuel related event, which occurred when the tugboat crew was off-loading POL into our south side fuel terminal. Somehow a Vietnamese crew member got splashed with a light grade of fuel, probably gasoline, and came into an ignition source.

Since all of the Vietnamese men smoked constantly, it was believed that either a co-worker or the victim caused the fire, which resulted in the man's death.

The fire was limited to a loose flange connection, and we used a dry chemical with water spray to kill the encircling flame impingement. A somewhat small fire with a tragic result.

I must mention that we had these occasional fires at our POL docks. The pipeline flanges were sometimes loosened by the Vietnamese to drip fuel into small containers for their personal use. Their carelessness usually caused a fire. It was hard to stop this type of illegal activity.

ASSISTING THE MEDICS

There were a couple of times when the medics called for our assistance. Two medical corpsman were assigned to each Army ambulance. Thus, if they became overwhelmed at an incident, they had their communications staff call us.

We would respond with the two lead engine companies and the rescue jeep, bringing twelve firefighters to the scene. Usually the PA&E fire chief and assistant chief would also respond.

Our worst personnel incident occurred when a fresh arrival of soldiers were standing formation at the 90th Replacement Battalion and an incoming rocket exploded in their midst. Upon arrival we all had our hands full doing what we could for these unfortunate soldiers who suffered a myriad of injuries. We used every battlefield dressing and bandage that we carried on the 530-Bs and from the Rescue jeep to treat these newly arrived soldiers.

The 90th was located not too far from Station 1. We felt the percussion when that particular rocket impacted the ground and shook our station's quarters. Our response was immediate, as we were all standing at the ready by our apparatus awaiting the bells.

THE PORT OF SAIGON AND THE DOCKS

Fires were a regular occurrence at the Port of Saigon and its docks. Everyone smoked back then, and many smokers were careless about the proper disposal of their respective smoking materials.

People did not care about their negative habits, so fires happened at all hours of the Port's operations. Saigon Fire Brigade probably went to the docks and the Port several times a month.

Several stubborn fires involved POL and other flammable liquids. Saigon Fire Brigade did not have any type of fire foam apparatus, nor any stockpiles of fire foam concentrate. They relied on us to assist when these incidents occurred. After all, it was United States war materials on fire.

Thus, the protein concentrate foam tender would make the long run to the Port of Saigon when a petroleum based fire occurred. Despite the best efforts of Saigon Brigade, there were times when only our fire foam could extinguish the uncontrollable blaze. LBFD was the expert here.

There were times that fires were burning inside the warehouses at the docks. And these were large serious fires. I regularly saw the two very powerful French pumpers, of which each were capable of pumping two thousand gallons of water per minute, operating at these incidents.

Again, these pumping engines delivered their water through large diameter hose that was six inches in diameter. I had never seen anything like this operating at a major fire stateside, nor was I even aware of such unique and powerful apparatus having been invented.

The huge volumes of water that were pumped came directly out of the South China Sea. These two pumpers simply backed up to the docks and dropped their hard suction hoses into the Port's body of water. Obviously, the water supply was endless, coming from the ocean.

I must mention that my first venture to the Port of Saigon and its docks was overwhelming to me. Staring in awe at the huge shipments of war materials coming in, and noticing the countless ships that were awaiting at anchor in the distance to offload, told me that this war was a big deal and big business. Seeing all of this left my young mind spinning.

The Port was full of military vehicles, and everything related to the support and sustainment of the overall war. There were more jeeps and 2-1/2 ton trucks than I could count. Of course, there were APCs, artillery, and tanks throughout the dock's laydown areas.

The Port was a beehive of activity. Countless workers and convoys of trucks were present, with all focused on supporting the war effort. Longshoremen were everywhere.

One very unusual sight were the railroad trains and their stacked trackage. They looked like oversized Lionel trains to me. The engines were all diesel powered, and there were plenty of boxcars, flatcars, and gondolas present awaiting their destination point. But the railroad track and ties assembly was what really impacted me. I could not believe what I was seeing.

The tracks were already pre-formed and stacked upon each other. These were a style of railroad tracks that were sectional and approximately fifty feet in length. They looked just like the tracks of a model Lionel train set. I was soon educated about this very progressive makeup.

These tracks were made with concrete ties arrayed over the long length of each sectional piece of rail. I was informed that wooden ties were no longer used because of the high water table of the landscape in Vietnam. The concrete ties resisted the constant wet conditions of their country in a superior manner over wooden ones. These pre-formed railroad track assemblies were easily transported to the railroad's route and roadbed, and simply joined together. Pretty clever!

Even the tracks that ran alongside of Highway 1 had this type of modernization. Vietnam was fortunate to have this modern approach to keeping their railways operating and somewhat successful, especially since the ground wetness and water table never diminished.

One final comment about the Port of Saigon. This is where the U. S. Merchant Marine brought and delivered to us our firefighting foam concentrate. With all of the petroleum based hazards that surrounded us, we would have been in great trouble knocking down these types of fires without foam. The Merchant Mariners were the best!

THE UNUSUAL AT SEA

Towards the end of my time in country, a most unusual request for our assistance took place.

There was a freighter anchored in the South China Sea several miles out from the Port of Saigon, and it was on fire. Evidently it had been burning for a while, and no one had the expertise, nor the proper equipment to respond. I also figured that no one wanted to be placed in harm's way.

It was fully loaded with war materials, and of course, it carried an unknown amount of munitions. It was a tall vessel, of which I believe was of a foreign registry, and smoking very heavily according to the Coast Guard, who were monitoring the ship.

Saigon Brigade did not have any specialized teams to venture out and handle the burning vessel. And the Port of Saigon did not have a fire boat. Thus, a call went out to us.

I told my crew about this alarm, and without hesitation everyone was eager to fight fire, despite none of us having any shipboard firefighting experience. We grabbed our battle gear and turnout clothing, and placed all of this on the engine.

The crew grabbed about twenty sections of the U. S. Naval pipe thread hose from Engine 6 and tossed it up on top of the hose bed with some extra nozzles, a gated wye, two fog applicators, and assorted hand tools.

I went to our shop area and grabbed several heat crayons from the welding rig. I figured I would smear the heat crayons on nearby bulkheads to determine how hot the temperatures were getting in the various holds once we got on the ship.

Thermal imagers were not invented then, and the only way we could determine what these heat conditions were, was to use the heat crayons and see if they melted into a runny wax type of appearance. Each crayon was colored differently and they were rated to melt at various temperatures.

I told the crew that hopefully the ship's fire pump would be in good working order, and that we could get all the water we needed to suppress the blaze. The only portable fire pump that we had was the P-250 unit that was mounted on the Tank.

We then mounted our 530-B, and we left for the Port from Gate One. It was about a 25 mile run for us, and we arrived safely without any traffic or negative interference on Highway One.

When we arrived at the docks, we could see the column of smoke on the eastern horizon of the South China Sea. We had our adrenaline going, and we were ready to fight the fire.

The on duty U. S. Coast Guard officer informed me that there was no way that his small boat could get us onto the vessel. It was simply too high, and the sea was full of waves with very visible white caps. He felt it was too risky for us to even try a rope ladder or the web netting for boarding the ship.

He said that MACV headquarters in Saigon was sending over a Huey for airborne transport to the burning ship. I asked him if the Huey's crew was going to land on the ship, and he thought that we probably would have to rappel onto the vessel.

I told my firemen that we might as well start making up our Swiss Seats, and to get the manila rope from the engine. We carried two coils of rope, and both were approximately two hundred feet in length. It was heavy rope, but that's what we used in those days. I believe that it was 5/8" in diameter.

The Huey arrived and we had a good briefing about getting onto the ship. The Huey's crew was going to spot us in a safe part of the deck, about one hundred feet or so above the vessel, and we were to rappel into that zone.

My driver/operator and I were the first to go. It was a bright sunny day, and as we got close to the burning ship, we became awestruck by the large volumes of smoke. I mentioned to him that this had to be something other than burning wooden crates of munitions, and he agreed.

The Huey maneuvered above the ship and we rappelled without incident onto the rear deck area of the stern. I was quickly met by the 1st Mate, who spoke excellent English, and started getting briefed by him as to what he felt was burning.

He stated that they had the majority of the ship's holds carrying uniforms. I was somewhat relieved that it appeared that no munitions were involved at this time. But overall, the burning supplies of uniforms was still going to give us a serious challenge,

He told me that the ship's Captain, and two other seamen were in the engine room with the ship's engineer ensuring that the fire pumps and their backups were in good working order. I told him that we brought our own hose and appliances, and that we just needed good water pressure of approximately one hundred pounds. He assured me that everything will be done to assist us.

The 1st Mate said that no one ever encountered a fire before, and that they were scared to death, and delighted to have us on board. He promised us a steak dinner and all the beer we could drink after we put out the fire. (We never got around to collecting this treat.)

Once the rest of our crew got on board, we assembled our firefighting tools and hooked up the hose lines. Then we handjacked everything over to the first hold where the smoke was the worst. As we readied our dual hose lines, the Captain, 1st Mate, and a seaman slowly lifted the hatch. We quickly opened our nozzles with the fog pattern and started our firefighting operations.

After a few minutes into the operation, I told the crew for them to keep one nozzle on the fog pattern, and the other to go straight stream. I then told the straight stream firemen to "rake" the nozzle back and forth, in the hopes of cutting into the fire and weakening its' resolve.

There was a tremendous volume of smoke and steam issuing forth as we initially attacked the fire. I really did not think we were having much of an effect on the burning holds, as it seemed to me that the fire was resisting our firefighting. But we were just young and stubborn, and felt that we would give the fire a challenge. After all, we were using our Navy nozzles, with one of them placed on a straight stream pattern at 150 pounds of pressure, through our 1-1/2" hose. To us that was outright brutal force from a fire hose stream! It took two of us to muscle the back-pressure for any period of time. And, yes, we were tired after this type of sustained forearm work!

Time passed and then the smoke finally started changing color. We knew that we were making progress. Soon the hatch was pulled open in a wider manner, and we could see and direct our fire streams towards the cardboard boxes that contained the uniforms which were burning.

We repeated this tactic to the other hold, and after about four hours of steady work, we found ourselves in complete control of killing the fires.

We stayed overnight on the ship, wetting down hot spots, and showed the ship's small crew how to operate the fire hoses and the correct manner of directing the water delivery.

During our lull in the battle, we were treated to some good food and sandwiches in the galley, and of course, cold Cokes.

The next day found us going over the side on the rope webbing, and jumping onto the Coast Guard boat to get back to the Port of Saigon. We were glad to complete this assignment and get back to Long Binh.

A ROAD ON FIRE

On one late afternoon the RTO called me over the PA and said to quickly report to the Alarm Room. I immediately went there and upon entering the room, I saw a look of disbelief on his face, with him still holding the fire phone handset.

He said that he had just received a phone call from the Engineer Unit, and that they were reporting that there was a road on fire next to the Post Exchange. I couldn't believe what I was hearing from the RTO.

I stepped outside and looked towards the eastside of the installation. There was a very visible and thin column of rich black smoke reaching for the sky.

I went back inside the Alarm Room and I asked the RTO what other information did he have regarding this call? He said "not much" except that the caller was pretty excited about the road being on fire, and to "come quickly".

I told the RTO to ring out all of Station 1's companies, including both foam units. He rang the house bell, and immediately afterwards sounded the klaxon. He also gave the address via the PA as the Post Exchange. Essentially this was the equivalent of a General Alarm for Station 1.

This action resulted in all five of our fire companies gearing up and responding at the same time, which was a rare event. We had to look like a fire engine parade going down the road.

While enroute to the location, we could see the growing column of thick black smoke in the distant atmosphere. It was also growing horizontally, and I knew that we had a working fire of some sort. I thought to myself now how could such a large fire occur during the daytime?

Something seriously had to be burning was what I was thinking in the cab of Engine 3 while we were enroute. I asked my driver "how could a road be on fire"? He was as puzzled as I was at that time. I noticed that he was seriously focused on his driving to get us there safely.

I was still trying to figure out how could a road be on fire as the 530-B roared over the main thoroughfare road to the Post Exchange? None of this made sense to me.

Upon our arrival we found that the roadway was truly on fire. The flames were a bright cherry red, and the radiating heatwaves were very hot. The accompanying smoke condition was dense and growing in volume against the skyline. Overall, it was a hostile and blistering fire to see!

I was greeted by two 46th Engineer officers, who told me that a fresh coating of PenePrime had just been applied to the roadway's surface. I also noticed that there was a roadway oil tanker truck parked off the shoulder of the road. So I knew what the challenge was going to be for us.

PenePrime is a very flammable substance in its liquid state. Once it becomes applied on an asphaltic road, and then cures, it remains as a stable sealer with no fire hazard condition.

What happened here was that a contractor Vietnamese tossed a still lit cigarette onto the oily wet grass adjacent to the road's shoulder. The PenePrime had just been freshly applied and was starting its curing process. Thus, it was still unstable and any open flame could cause it to ignite.

This careless act became the ignition source and it immediately started the fire.

We had both lanes of the road on fire, and it extended about a quarter of a mile. It was pretty scary for everyone to see in the broad daylight. The fire was blazing quite fiercely and the smoke production was downright nasty and voluminous. One could not believe their eyes!

Engine 4's crew was already pulling their pre-connected lines with the High-Ex foam nozzles attached, and were getting ready to charge their lines. I told them to hold up.

I then said to Engine 3's crew to pull both boosters, and go up in the crow's nest with them. I had the driver move the truck to the unburned roadway shoulder, and said to him to engage the PTO for a "Pump'n'Roll" operation. I also told him to use the low transfer case for higher rpm to increase the water pressure results when they started moving.

I went over to the middle of the rig and briefed the two firefighters in the crow's nest to aim their nozzles at the burning roadway and use a "Powercone" pattern against the flames. I also told my driver to stay on the unburned shoulder of the road and move slowly with the engine.

The rig started to move, and as the hose lines engaged the flames, they quickly started killing that portion of the fire. The sudden production and atmospheric liberation of steam and hydroscopic vapor was pretty intense from the reaction of the booster streams' water upon the burning roadway. This was very good firefighting over all, as the positive return here was that the firefighters were knocking down the flames progressively with no flashback or rekindle.

Engine 3's crew kept up this offensive maneuver for the entire quarter mile, and soon they had all of the fire completely extinguished. Fortunately, 400 gallons of booster water was enough.

Engine 4's foam crew remained at the ready, and was not needed. A modest water spray knocked down the fire to go below its ignition temperature. The burning PenePrime sealer oil was cooled effectively, thereby stopping the blaze. And again we were lucky with success.

The Engineers' cadre' of officers and their NCOs were amazed and delighted that we were able to stop the blaze. Of course, I am sure that they had some tough questions to answer about this fire to their Command within the hour, but at least we looked good!

GRASS FIRES

Despite Vietnam having a very green landscape of vegetation, with adequate rainfall, we were still plagued with occasional grass fires. And some of these fires, if not attended to promptly, could lead to a serious fire loss destroying nearby valuable war materials and/or buildings.

Most of these grass and vegetation fires were the result of carelessly discarded smoking material.

Just about everyone smoked back then, and tossing your butts out on the grass was both irresponsible and yet commonplace. So even in a war zone, fire prevention was not in the forefront of things. The war had plenty of other distractions occupying one's primary thoughts.

A serious fire can be a diversion before or during a battle. The Roman army showed us how they used fire as a weapon of war many centuries ago. It worked, and it worked very well for them.

Usually these fires were the result of an act of carelessness, and if the ground conditions were dry, then a hot blaze quickly ensued. If there was a good breeze blowing, then there was further concern about this just being an ordinary grass fire. A small fire could grow rapidly unchecked.

The laydown yard for the 55 gallon drum storage of PenePrime was a major fire loss for the Army while I was there. It resulted from a minor grass fire not being reported quickly. As the flames moved across the grass, the fire found a leaking drum, and soon the whole inventory was going up in a mammoth conflagration. This became one of Long Binh's worst fires on record.

I have reported on this particular fire earlier in this writing, as it beat me up pretty well during that unforgiving encounter. It was one of the hottest fires that I can remember.

I must also comment on the use of nighttime flares. Our troops used a mechanical airborne chemical flare, with a small parachute, to illuminate the ground whenever enemy troop activity was suspected. These flares were also used if something suspicious was getting close to our base perimeter.

They basically were a bright white chemical burning light that floated slowly to the ground via their attached parachutes. They worked pretty well for lighting up a given area, so our troops could see if there was any forthcoming enemy threat, under the glare of the airborne device.

Once in a while, the chemical flare continued to burn beyond its given life span, and would remain lit when it touched the ground. These were imperfect chemical mixes, so yes, it did happen often. Thus, a quickly ignited grass or brush fire was the result if left unchecked.

We would get a fire call on these mishaps from our well-meaning, yet already nervous troops, who were standing guard on the installation perimeter. And it made good sense to call us, since any unattended grass or brush fire could quickly escalate to a major blaze, and head for a critical piece of military war material or building.

Any of our small ammo bunkers, which were scattered throughout the installation, were of immediate concern to us. They were earth covered and usually had a good natural vegetation cover. So a fire was an easy prey upon these ordnance storage facilities.

We responded to these fires without any delay. We were highly concerned to stop them as soon as possible, as no one wanted to have a loss of our military ordnance and munitions.

Most of the time they were easy to extinguish with a stream from one of the booster lines. Flaps, shovels, and rakes were also used on the inside of our fence lines when the brush was thick.

We took our responses and everything very seriously about grass and brush fires.

RIOTS AND FIRES AT LONG BINH JAIL

I mentioned earlier that Long Binh Jail was quite the noted institution of the entire installation. I think it even overshadowed the good fame that the Bob Hope Show brought to the amphitheater.

Its inhabitants contributed negatively to every infamous activity. And in a war zone, it's hard to fathom how and why professional soldiers would choose to conduct themselves in committing such various and serious crimes. Their corrupt actions reduced their rank to that of inmate.

Having a lifelong record follow them was unavoidable, and many went to Fort Leavenworth for lifetime sentences. Plus the temptation of the Black Market prospects caused many a downfall.

The MPs detailed there were true correctional officers and very dedicated. They even received different training from what the other MP cadre' of soldiers attained during their AIT.

Because of the unique nature of the prison, and what they had to do in their duties, these MPs were always challenged. I have to salute them for their never ending cycle of duty at LBJ.

Even their MOS number was different from the MPs who were stationed across the roadway from our Central Station. It had to be a job that eventually wore you down.

In all of my dealings with the correctional MPs, I found them to be very professional and helpful to the firefighters during our responses to LBJ.

Some of our responses involved mattress and bedding fires. Usually these were the result of smoking, although having a cigarette or other smoking material was considered pure contraband within the prison's confines. It didn't matter anyway, as the Black Market with its unsavory friends of the inmates found ways to supply them with a little bit of everything forbidden.

Usually these fires were somewhat more hazy and sooty, with little visible flame, but producing and sending a fair volume of smoke throughout the nearby cell areas of the prison. These smoke conditions seriously impeded the MPs overall vision of the holding areas, and thus these fires and incidents always required us to immediately transport the burning item(s) away from the prison's interior to an open yard to knock down the fire. (Synthetics burned stubbornly.)

Sometimes we just let these things burn freely in the yard outside the prison, as water and even firefighting foam was ineffective against the burning mattress or bedding material.

There were a couple of times that actual large scale riots occurred, with inmates fighting each other, and/or the MPs. Sometimes fires were set in conjunction with the rioting, and while they were burning out of control, the general instability of overall prison security was a concern.

All of us felt uncomfortable when these riots occurred, as they were extremely serious events to the security and stability of the prison, which would have echoed throughout all of Long Binh.

First of all, it was downright scary to see the MPs going at it with the inmates through the barbed wire and hurricane fencing, and many an

MP took a beating in the process. We stayed outside the sally port until the MP's OIC or NCOIC felt it was safe for us to enter the compound.

We only committed one truck to the inside prison yard. If there was a requirement for a sustained water supply to fight the fire(s), then we handjacked a single 2-1/2" hose line through a nearby suitable gate or the sally port to provide the large volume needed for fire suppression.

There were no hydrants installed around the prison. We had to tender all of the required water. It was a basic nursing operation for us. One engine fed the supply line to the inside fire company or their engine, and the tenders supplied the exterior pumping apparatus until the fire was out.

During one nasty incident a small structure was set on fire. It was located about seventy feet away from the perimeter of the prison fence lines. I believe that it held cleaning supplies and tools, like brooms and numerous related items. Fortunately for us we were able to knock down the flames fairly quickly upon our arrival with a long range stream outside the fence.

We were able to position our lead engine next to the fence line and using the straight bore solid tip stream from a 1-1/2" Navy nozzle, we easily killed the fire with this long range attack. The firefighters who directed the fire stream positioned themselves in the crow's nest of the 530-B. It gave them an excellent vantage point to deluge the building with a powerful flow of water.

There were quiet periods at LBJ for everyone. This usually occurred when a large segment of their society was transported back to the states for trial and further incarceration. The reduction of the prison population resulted in a quiet calm overall.

Every one of us welcomed the lull in this environment, and I am sure that the MPs were as equally relieved.

THE DUMP AND THE BURNING PIT FIRES

Long Binh had both a dump for waste and trash, and a burning pit for destroying a wide variety of material.

We were a true military city with all of the negative activities that follow us through life. Having a trash dump was part of it all. The burning pit was the incinerator.

The dump was remotely located, and the local Vietnamese were permitted access to search and reclaim the trash for their use through a monitored and guarded gate. PA&E ran this part of the operation.

Aluminum cans were in high demand. The Vietnamese used to cut open the can lids and bottoms, and flatten out the sidewalls. They used the flat metal pieces to serve as exterior walls and roofing material for their little shack homes. It was quite a sight to see these little houses constructed and covered with Lone Star and Black Label markings. Seemed to work pretty well for them, as overall the local population were poor, and welcomed anything of useful value.

Tires and scrap pieces of rubber and plastic were also in great demand. The local Vietnamese fashioned a "thong" style of walking shoe from these materials. They were pretty clever in making practical items from our waste.

Sometimes we were called for a nuisance fire at the dump. We would play out the booster tank and sometimes use all of the 1200 gallons from the tender to knock down some of the nasty burning conditions. All we really did was create another smoky mess, but the Vietnamese were happy that we killed the flames so they could re-enter the dump areas, and search for whatever they wanted. The Vietnamese did not seem to mind the smoke, just the open flame conditions.

Seems like there was always something burning under the huge piles of trash and waste. It would have taken heavy equipment to unearth these smoldering fires, and thus it would have become an endless cycle of nuisance fire chasing for us. I believe that we went there about two or three times a month to knock down any runaway fire or open flame situation.

Sometimes we just sent two men and a water tender, as one could only do so much. There was always going to be a fire at the dump, and we did not want to shortchange our fire services and levels of protection, which might be urgently needed elsewhere on the installation.

The Vietnamese always smiled and waved their hands at us as we were leaving after knocking down any of the fires. They shouted "Thank you Cuu Hoa!" in their best English.

It should be noted that the master burning pit was used by both GI and PA&E personnel to destroy various items, commodities, and paper material via open flame. I know that several units throughout Long Binh had their own small burn pit to destroy documents and related sensitive information within their immediate facilities. We did not interfere with any of these activities.

FUNNY FIRES

Every now and then we would get a call from some unit on Long Binh that an outhouse was on fire. And sure enough, upon our arrival, there would be a well-burning outhouse.

What happened here, was usually a combination of awkward factors, which caused the actual fire to occur. Careless smoking inside the outhouse was one culprit for ignition. And then...

A "newbie" soldier would be assigned to "burn the shitter" as commanded by his company officer or NCO. This uninformed newly arrived soldier would then proceed to light off the wooden structure after giving it a good splash and soaking of MoGas.

He should have opened the lower back door of the outhouse and removed the sawed-off 55 gallon drum half to an open area of the yard. Then he was to have applied diesel fuel, with a little spiking of gasoline and ignite it, thereby "burning the shitter" of its waste.

I can only imagine what extra work details were assigned this unfortunate soldier when his command called him to the front office after the fire.

If he did not have any carpenter skills beforehand, then he quickly learned how to construct a new wooden outhouse. Some of these units

THE NEGATIVE SIDE OF FUNNY FIRES

I would be remiss here if I did not report on the negative side of this section of "Funny Fires", and it involves the actual burning of human waste via this method.

These events of burning human waste occurred on a daily basis and this was all confined to any given company's yard. Several drum halves could be on fire at once. The smoke condition would linger and if one was downwind, it was absolutely noxious to inhale.

The barracks at Long Binh were not air conditioned. Windows had open screens and fans were the only cooling system that the GI's had. So it would be very easy for the smoke to drift into anyone's quarters. Any foreign odor could quickly penetrate a soldier's personal quarters.

I can remember stories about personnel complaining of the stubborn odor that would prevail within their quarters for several days. Every now and then we would be visited at the station by a lower rank enlisted soldier, who inquired about how to get the smoke odor out of their rooms.

were multi-stalls, which meant that three to five seats were in each structure. And yes, these were sizable structures for one man to build.

Of course he would be the subject delight of various jokes and clever remarks as he would be building the replacement unit in broad daylight on the open yard of the respective military unit.

I would have to note and remark about how such an event would figure into a returning veteran's war stories. Would it be something funny to share with all for a good laugh, or would one just be too embarrassed to say anything at all?

We recommended the old-time method of placing open dishes of vinegar around to neutralize the smoke smell and odor. I don't think that worked at all. We also never heard back from anyone after offering this advice to neutralize the smoke odor condition in their quarters if it worked.

To breathe in burning products of combustion, with untreated human waste, had to raise some kind of havoc on anyone's overall health. And with long term consequences to follow. My own personal breathing difficulty issues are daily challenges. The chronic after-effects are real.

The drums were usually brought to a stage of agitated boiling and the smoke production was quite prevalent. The fires never were hot enough to completely destroy the contents. After a drum halve burned out, the slop was usually tossed into a nearby open ditch.

I am sure that many soldiers got sick from the combination of these negative and polarizing combined atmospheres. Like any inhalation of the products of combustion, there was not only numerous and immediate negative effects, but there had to be long-term afflictions as well.

Any burning process is imperfect and this system was outright putrid. There is always going to be minute toxic material that can be inhaled and absorbed by one's health system. The future is unknown as to how anyone's health attributes will combat these negative entries into the body.

One other item to note is the fact that these metal 55 gallon drums were never checked for what toxic chemicals or other hazardous liquids might have been inside. Everyone just assumed that if one could not see any hazard, then there was no hazard. As we know now, numerous chemicals are the bane of our society regarding chronic health conditions and premature death.

And I truly believe that my lung issues and ongoing overall health challenges are directly connected here. All of my doctors also agree with the fact that firefighters without SCBA would be subject to a negative chronic health problem. The newly enacted legislation of the PACT Act now gives factual credence that these issues are real, and that the VA can take care of those of us who were negatively affected.

A RECAP OF THE PENEPRIME FIRES

I wrote about a couple of items regarding the PenePrime fires earlier in this document. I wish to explain in further detail how serious and downright ferocious these fires were to us.

First off, PenePrime is composed of pure hydrocarbon elements. It is a black liquid, with a strong odor of elemental hydrocarbon. One immediately knows that this is a serious odor and smell that slaps you quickly into an unknown state of trouble. If you have ever passed an oil refinery on a bright sunny day, and the wind is blowing your direction, then you can have a general idea of what a powerful hydrocarbon smell is.

One cannot mistake this unique substance once you have smelled it the first time. It is an unforgettable attack upon your senses. Even your eyes will smart from the atmosphere of being in the association of PenePrime.

PenePrime is basically an asphalt sealer. It behaves in a "rubberized" fashion once it becomes cured upon any given roadway. The heavy tonnage of vehicular traffic wears down asphaltic roads quickly. The application of PenePrime acts both as a sealer, and as a stabilizer to the premature cracking and "alligatoring" of the roadway's surface.

Unfortunately for us, PenePrime gave us serious challenges during the two major blazes that we encountered. The resulting fires were brutal and tested us beyond our normal limits in both firefighting and complete suppression. Essentially, one of the fires just burned itself out.

Once the liquid base of PenePrime becomes ignited, there is no turning back of the dynamic combustion chain reaction. The fires take on an almost supernatural behavior of flame and smoke production. The smoke alone can color the sky from blue to black within moments.

The understatement here is that we never faced such a flaming dragon during our time in country. When the PenePrime caught fire, it took on a mind of its own, ignored our best suppression efforts, and it ran like wild beast, ignoring any firefighting effort!

These fires burned in an ultra-hot manner, giving off blistering waves of radiated heat, and the overall smoke production was enormous and conflagration like.

Our fire streams had little to no effect upon the way these fires burned. Even with fire streams being fed a foam concentrate mixture of 6%, little was accomplished to kill the burning process.

At the laydown yard, where well over a couple hundred drums of PenePrime was stored and burning, we gave up throwing firefoam at the blaze. We could see it disappearing before our eyes, and having no effect upon the PenePrime. We did not want to waste this limited resource of our fire foam concentrate stockpile. We reverted back to water streams.

All of the soldier-firefighters suffered from burns, dehydration, and smoke inhalation during these firefighting missions. It depended upon where you worked the fire, as to what your injuries could be. Remember, there was no relief nor rehab breaks for us. One just worked until the blaze was extinguished, and then restoring our equipment came next. Mission first!

All of us agreed that the smoke inhalation was the worst injury, as one was breathing not only the smoke, but the "off-gassing" of the raw hydrocarbon itself. You got sick quickly from all of this toxic mixture. Vomiting was one's only relief when you met your inhalation limit. And you were dizzy for another good twelve to twenty four hours afterwards, plus having a nasty headache that aspirin could not touch. Inhaling oxygen helped sometimes. But not always.

Burned and unburned products of the combustion process directly wreaked havoc upon all of our health mechanisms. I can only imagine that our youth kept us going during these periods of unforgiving firefighting encounters.

We even tried our "Silvers" during our first blaze to ward off the high heat levels. They did not help our level of personal protection. The Silvers got exceptionally hot within five to ten minutes, and the members wearing them started jumping around and couldn't get out of them fast enough. Even the enclosed hoods became intolerable from absorbing so much radiated heat.

After these fires took place, everyone involved felt it was a surreal event. All realized that it was a very serious experience, not just for the firefighters, but for the installation's personnel too.

Without question, PenePrime became highly respected and regarded, just like Class 1 Ordnance.

Numerous safety procedures and plans were developed and instituted by the Post Engineers and PA&E contractors regarding the handling, storage, and application of PenePrime. After these new measures were in place, we experienced no further challenges.

THE GENERAL WESTMORELAND RELATIONSHIP

The world is a small place at times, and I would be remiss if I did not share this unique bond to General Westmoreland. After all, he was the supreme commander for the Vietnam conflict, and everyone serving in the allied forces of Vietnam had tremendous respect for his leadership and skill. He was truly a soldier's soldier!

My first encounter with General Westmoreland started when we would greet his aircraft at the USARV Headquarters landing pad when he came on in from Saigon.

Our lead fire crew stood at the ready should a mishap occur with our 530-B and the 1200 gallon water tender. We did not want a second to elapse should something go wrong. The crew stood there until the aircraft, always a rotary wing, was safely secure on the tarmac.

We also returned for his departure flight back to his command quarters in Saigon. I always rendered a salute to him from my position outside the front of the 530-B whenever the aircraft landed or took off. I was dressed in my "silvers" and had my red crew chief's helmet on.

One day while I was standing by the front of the rig as his aircraft landed, a Captain came over to me, and said the General wanted to see me before we left. I said "yes Sir!" and followed the Captain back to the entrance of USARV Headquarters.

I was somewhat shook up as I felt that I was in trouble for something. Within a minute of waiting, I was escorted to see the General in his office, and upon entering I found him to be very welcoming and cordial. I was immediately relieved, fearing earlier that big trouble was coming my way.

He said that he was told that I was an accomplished musician, who played the organ in church back home, and at the main post chapel for special occasions. I told the General that his information was correct.

The General then said would I be willing to play appropriate wedding ceremony music for one of his aides, who was of a Captain rank? He went on to say that it would be a Catholic wedding at the Main Post Chapel on Long Binh. I told him that it would be a great honor for me. General Westmoreland was pleased and said that his staff would brief me later with the details.

Here's the rest of the story and yes, it happened in a war zone.

The young Captain fell in love with one of the PA&E contractor secretaries. Thus, they did not want to wait any longer, and permission was granted for them to tie the knot.

The day came, which was a Saturday, and I played several pieces of wedding music for their ceremony, which was a Catholic Mass by the way. The 530-B was parked outside, and the fire crew took a back row of pews for the duration of the event. Wish I had pictures of this to share!

I did have one last encounter with the General while I was still in country, and that was at the Bob Hope Show. Bob Hope and his entourage came and performed their 1970 Christmas week show at the Long Binh Amphitheater that December. I greeted the General when his command car arrived at the rear of the stage, and then he went to the front to enjoy the entertainment.

Engine 3's crew had the coveted standby duty for backstage protection of the electrical sound system and equipment. Dean Martin's "Ding-a-Ling" girls were the hot point of the show for all of the GIs. Everyone thoroughly enjoyed seeing these little beauties dance and sing for us, and yes, they were really pretty!

But my story doesn't end here.

Time marches on and I find myself attending the annual Department of Defense Fire & Emergency Services (FES) conference in Dallas, Texas in August of 2000. All of the military branches' FES chief officers and key staff members were in attendance. Little did I know the wonderful surprise that was to come my way from participating at this event!

There were two hotels that co-hosted our entourage, that were built on the Dallas Fort Worth (DFW) airport property. And unknown to us, these hotels also had the annual Medal of Honor (MOH) conference going on at the same time. Essentially the MOH members were co-located with all the military and Federal fire chiefs.

Since the inception of the combination of all of the FES branches into one major training conference, I became and was responsible as a steering committee member for the Army's participation and contributions for a successful outcome.

My duties included serving as the master musician, chaplain, and overall ceremony and protocol guidance chairman. I was in the direct administrative line of reporting to the Director of Army Fire Services at the Pentagon. Never a dull moment during these conferences for me.

I had just finished one briefing for the awards night banquet, and left the breakout room to go across the main lobby to another meeting. There I saw a number of MOH personnel and several were gathered around General Westmoreland in the main concourse of the lobby. All were dressed in civilian clothes, including the General. But, one could easily see him as he usually towered above everyone, being of height well over six foot tall.

I was in my Class B chief's uniform, and the General took notice of me as I started moving his direction. I was watching the small group, and the next thing I saw was the General's hand motioning for me to come his way. I slightly changed my direction, and went over to him and the MOH fellows.

We shook hands and exchanged greetings. Then the General says to me, "a fire chief"? I answered "yes, General." Then he said "where do I know you from"? I told him that I was the fire crew chief from Long Binh, Vietnam, who stood by his aircraft whenever he came to USARV Headquarters, and that I was the organist for the young Captain's wedding.

The General broke into the biggest smile and said to me "I remember the big eyebrows". We enjoyed a good laugh, and then spent some time visiting about Long Binh, and where did my Army career take off to.

He was genuinely concerned about my well-being, and said to reach out to him for anything he could do for me.

We wished each other well, and overall it was a blessing to see him and visit once again.

TOUCHING HOME VIA HAM RADIO

Since cell phones were not invented yet, and the global telephone system did not possess the international ease of reaching out to anyone in the world, the in-country military personnel could use the assistance of numerous HAM radio operators to make a call home.

Countless HAM radio operators volunteered their time and equipment to help us make a phone call home via their worldwide system. They truly and silently supported us in the war, despite what the rest of America felt, by sharing their talents.

The only cost involved was the long distance connection from the home base telephone line of the HAM operator to where you wanted to call. The cost was a collect, of course, to your home and/or loved ones line.

Overall, it was a bargain, and a real treat to hear each other's voices. It felt like Christmastime!

At most of the installations and bases in Vietnam, and the handful of USO clubs, there was usually a HAM radio base station and a qualified operator. (The operator was a military communications specialist.) So one could place a call without too much effort.

Timing was everything, as there were numerous other soldiers awaiting their opportunity also.

When you got your turn, you placed a headset over your ears, and spoke into the microphone. As soon as you finished speaking, then you had to say the word "Over". This command meant for the operator at the other end to switch to the transmit mode, while your set got switched to receive.

Of course, whoever you were speaking to also had to use this command word to ensure that the radio wave would be carrying your voice in the right direction. It worked flawlessly.

None of us abused this system. We restricted ourselves to a call a month per firefighter. We realized that everyone needed an open moment to call home.

This system and method permitted us to reach out quickly if something happened here or even back home. We did have the workings of the United States Military Postal Service available to us, but the average delivery time of a letter from Vietnam to the States took about two weeks.

The HAM radio operators were great Patriots and true heroes to all of us!

R 'N' R AND AN UNSUITABLE ENDING

One "treat" that was given to all who served in country was a one week get-away to a safe location, called R 'n' R. And it did not impact your built up leave time. Rest and Relaxation was the translation for R 'n' R.

This was basically a limited trip to a friendly locale, to receive a brief respite from our war duties. One qualified for it after serving three months in country.

Some of the locations were Singapore, Tokyo, Australia, Hawaii, and Thailand.

Most of us took it at the halfway mark. I took mine around the three-quarter timeframe. This was due to the fact that I wanted to go to Hawaii and see my folks. The deciding factor was that the major airlines offered half price fairs to parents to come and meet their family member in Hawaii.

So my Mom and Dad got things together, and we were in Hawaii during Thanksgiving. It was great overall, but a negative event happened on the last day we were together.

Many military personnel came to Hawaii to enjoy themselves with family and/or girlfriends. All of the military R'n'R participants were being watched by the local crime thugs. This element of criminal activity lurked in the shadows following everyone's movements and lifestyle.

Dad booked us at the Royal Hawaiian Hotel. It was nice, and upscale. We all figured that we would be safe and secure staying there. There appeared to be nothing amiss.

We went out to lunch on the last day together, and upon returning to our room, we were greeted by a mess. Evidently a very bold forced entry was made to our room. Our bags were ripped open, and our cameras were stolen. Several other nice articles of clothing were also gone.

The sad fact was that our cameras were in their travel cases, and numerous rolls of undeveloped film was also stored alongside the cameras. Thus, the theft resulted in many fire scene shots and unusual fire activity photos being lost forever.

Surprisingly, the robbers did not take the new pairs of leather gloves, hand lanterns, and flashlights that I purchased for several of the men. Some dumb luck here.

The police came immediately and worked things, but these thugs were well ahead of the cops.

The investigating officers could not believe that a daylight robbery took place in an upscale location. This was a first for them in a fine hotel setting. The senior officer felt real bad for us, and he worked this case for a couple of years, but to no avail.

The hotel's manager was visibly upset, and when we checked out, he did not charge my Dad for the room. At least it was some consolation for our loss.

FILM, PHOTOS AND POLAROIDS

Lots of photos were taken by everyone who was interested in capturing their participation in the war. I wanted to have some photographic memories myself, thus I eventually purchased both a 35mm camera, and a Polaroid camera at the Long Binh Post exchange.

Of course the rules said to not take photos of critical areas and equipment, but it did not stop certain GIs from doing so. Some would get caught when they sent their 35mm film off to be developed. The PX had a lab in Japan where one could send their rolls of film. Usually the turnaround time was prompt. In about two weeks the developed film would be in your mailbox.

Polaroids were very popular at that time despite their higher cost. One had instant satisfaction and no security issues to deal with. The PX sold thousands of film packs for this process.

The majority of the photographs in this book are Polaroids.

THE FIREHOUSE MASCOT

One hardly ever saw a dog or a cat when one was in country. The exception was the Military Working Dogs (MWD). The MWD's talents were used for various missions, especially to support the MPs and some of the "tunnel rat" squads. These dogs were trained for a wide variety of specific purposes.

Now in regards to the absence of the ordinary street and village animals, we were told that these animals became food and considered a "specialty" when served. Of course, we were all repulsed upon hearing this.

Assistant Chief Cha did find a stray dog out roaming around one day, and he brought the dog back to his off post living quarters. He said that the dog was very skinny at first and was nervous. Soon the dog started gaining some weight and his mannerisms calmed down. He was a quiet dog, and never barked.

Eventually the dog came to the firehouse, and became a permanent part of our family. Cha gave the dog an unassuming name of "Ricky". Ricky quickly adopted to our way of life, and despite not being trained, he never left the confines of the fire station property. I guess his dog sense told him that he was safe in the firehouse and around all of us.

Ricky and I soon became buddies. I would speak to him and scratch his head. Once in a while I would bring some scraps from the mess hall, when we had a lull in our action, and give him a treat of people food.

When I left for home, Ricky watched me pack, and had his eyes glued on me. I guess he knew that his buddy was going somewhere. He backed his body into a corner of the apparatus floor when I got into the Jeep, and just stared at me until we each became small dots in the distance.

HOLIDAYS AND SPECIAL OCCASIONS

A traditional holiday was just another day for us. They came and went. All we wanted to celebrate was the fact that we were another day closer to going home.

One of the Vietnamese firemen brought some Christmas decorations for the 1970 season. They were strung out at our outside patio area, which was actually our covered training spot for classroom sessions. It gave us some hope that we would be celebrating our next Christmas in the states with our loved ones.

Birthdays were simply celebrated by having a cookout on our homemade grill in the evening, and praying for no runs during this timeframe. And washing down the meal with a beer.

We repeated this when one of us left country. Basically a simple celebration that one of us made it to go home in one piece.

HAIL & FAREWELL WITH THE VIETNAMESE FIREFIGHTERS

Approximately two weeks before I left Long Binh for the States, I was asked by a couple of the PA&E contract Vietnamese firefighters to be their guest at their homes for a farewell meal and reception.

I asked my chain of command, and received permission to go. I did not know what to expect upon my arrival and entrance to their little modest homes.

When I entered their homes, the first thing that I noticed was a wall that had a collection of mounted photographs and a table with burning incense and candles. It was a family shrine and considered a sacred part of their home.

This was a place of honor for them. The overall display was made up of their family and friends who served and fought in the war. Many were still on active duty, and these families were proud of them and their ongoing military service in the South Vietnamese armed forces.

Some of the photos had a black ribbon attached, and it meant that this person gave their life for their country.

I also learned that many Vietnamese were of the Christian Faith. There were the traditional Buddhists, but overall Christianity had made its mark throughout South Vietnam.

After viewing all of this and having things explained to me in further detail, it really made a very serious impact upon my understanding of the complete war effort.

I came to grips to fully understand how difficult fighting Communism had been for South Vietnam and its countrymen. And this war had been going on for years in their country. Well before the United States got involved.

These people were true patriots for their cause of sustained democracy. Their sacrifices were indeed great.

THE BIG HAIL & FAREWELL WITH THE PA&E CHIEF FIRE OFFICERS

The weekend before I was to come home was set aside on that Saturday night for my official Hail & Farewell with the fire department. I really could not believe that I was going to go home.

I must admit that I had some misgivings about leaving the unique bonds that I had established with the PA&E Fire Chiefs, and the contract Vietnamese Firefighters. We came to respect each other, and we all knew that something about serving as firefighters together was a noble cause, despite our differences and nationalities.

All five of the PA&E chiefs were there, which included the Korean assistant chief. Two of the off duty Vietnamese fire crew chiefs attended, and both of the Vietnamese secretaries also. The event was held at an off-post restaurant that Chief Petersen knew about, which was in a safe area and served great food.

The food was a venison steak with all the trimmings, and it was almost like being back in the USA, as it tasted delicious.

Beer, good conversation, and laughter consumed the evening. At the end of the meal, several nice comments were made in my presence, and at the conclusion of the remarks, I was presented with a firefighter's wall plaque that was uniquely Vietnamese.

What I really like about this plaque is that all of the chiefs' names are inscribed upon it. I miss them all, and I was greatly honored to have served alongside each one of them. I trust that hopefully a blessing will happen one day when we can see each other in Elysium.

I must mention that the senior chief at the event was Tom Brantley, and he always cared for me as if I was his son. His thoughtful guidance and brilliant wisdom was always welcome to me as a young firefighter. I will always treasure his warm smile and cordial greeting whenever he came down to Long Binh, and we had a chance to "talk shop".

Without question, he had a most remarkable and special surprise for me.

It was a very small package. When I opened it up, I found it to be a gold-filled miniature fire chief's badge. He took it upon himself to work behind the scenes with PA&E's management staff and his brother fire chiefs to see that I was made an Honorary PA&E Fire Chief!

I have proudly displayed this treasured memento throughout the years in my firefighting collection of memorabilia.

And yes, it's real gold, as it has never tarnished in its case!

I must say that Chief Brantley was a rock-solid mentor to me. He certainly was a true professional of the Old School, and a Gentleman of the Fire Service!

COMING HOME

The day finally arrived and I was taken from Fire Station 1 to Tan Son Nhut airbase in Saigon for my return to the States. The Korean PA&E Contractor Assistant Chief Cha drove me there, and it was difficult to say goodbye to him. I learned so much from him, and not just about firefighting, but many common sense ways of dealing with tough times and decisions. I was fortunate to have him as my "battle-buddy" during my time at the fire department.

Of course I already had my papers in my hand from the previous day to muster out. I got on the plane, and once it was airborne, the flight was quiet and peaceful.

All aboard were thankful to start our journey home. I believe all of us were still in shock that we were going home, and I am sure that many silent prayers were being said.

I must mention at this time that my orders to go home were paid for by another MOS' money. Even though I was a 51M, the orders showed a 21M processing payment code. It seems like the firefighter was so limited in numbers, that funding was shifted to take care of us.

We had a short stop in Tokyo, as we were to change planes for the final leg to California. I spent a couple of hours drifting around the main terminal, and purchased a nice camera tripod at one of the gift shops. (Yes, I still have that high quality item, and use it regularly.)

Soon the stateside flight was ready for us to board. That final flight from Tokyo took us to San Francisco for final clearance and our ETS.

We were treated to a steak meal upon our arrival at the Army Processing Center, and issued Class "B" clothing for our dress to wear going home. Most of us really didn't care what to wear officially, as we had been awake for nearly 24 hours, and we were getting tired, plus the jet lag was taking its toll also.

Of course, there were several Army recruiters' desks on location, of which we had to pass by on our exit from the out-processing facility. They were there to give us "one last chance" of reconsidering a career in the Army. Most of us (all Vietnam veterans now) quickly "double-timed" as we passed the desks. Pretty much everyone had enough of the Army life in Vietnam. I had one recruiter, a senior NCO, call out to me, and so I stopped and listened to him.

The recruiter noted that I was a firefighter, and he said that the Army always has great respect for our MOS. Well, that really caught my attention! Thus, he went on to tell me that I could be made a hard-stripe E-5 today, and within six months be promoted to E-6. Wow, I thought what's going on here!

He explained that there was limited rank and structure to remain in the Army firefighting career, and I already knew that, so what he said to me next did take me by surprise.

The recruiter said for me to change my MOS of Firefighting to EOD. EXPLOSIVE ORDANCE DISPOSAL! Those words were nowhere in my young mind. I was stuck in my tracks at that moment. And I paused for several minutes, and then took a chair next to his desk. I sat down, and I went into a deep thought, and actually felt pretty "cool" about that offer.

This senior NCO kept on selling me about how the Army knows that firefighters were brave and daring, and yet could work very hazardous events with a great outcome. He said we displayed calm thinking and were practical performers in a variety of skills. Thus, according to him, we were ideal candidates for EOD.

He was really convincing overall, and I started having second thoughts about leaving the Army behind. Then my memory kicked in and reminded me that things were waiting for me back home. Music and a civil service career were the advent at my doorstep.

I told him that these two careers were on the horizon already and I thanked him for his time and explanation. He said that I could muster back in within the month if I changed my mind. I just had to visit a local recruiting office.

My final flight home was from San Francisco to Moline, Illinois, with a stopover in Denver. At the old Denver International Airport, I had to depart the plane for another carrier. I also had about four hours to wait out. Thus I drifted around the terminal, hoping that time passed quickly.

During that timeframe I became hungry, and went to the sole snack bar. I was in uniform, and must have been a sight with my extremely deep suntan. All of us vets looked like we spent a couple of weeks tanning at a resort. I stood at the front counter and no one would wait on me. In fact, most folks didn't say two words to any of us during our layover time there.

Finally after about ten minutes or so passed by, an elderly black woman noticed me from the back of the snack bar, and come up to the front counter. (She had been preparing sandwiches in the back.) She said that several of her kinfolk were serving in Vietnam, and asked me what menu item would I like to have? I ordered one hot dog and a Coke, which she quickly got for me. I thanked her for waiting on me, and she wished me a safe journey home.

Soon it was boarding time, and a few of us got on the final leg of our journey home. I must say that the aircrews and staff were all nice to us ever since we left Vietnam. The stewardesses and pilots all said

"Hello" and welcomed us to their plane. It was the only real and sincere reception that we received during our travels.

Fortunately no one experienced any war protestors or negative events that could have been directed towards us during our air travel and ground time. I guess we were lucky since the majority of our travel time occurred at night.

Upon my return home, I got off the plane at the airport in Moline, Illinois, and was joyously greeted by my parents, grandmother, and my two younger sisters.

It was surreal for me, as I could not believe that I was safe and alive, and felt somehow that I had to go back, as this wonderful time with my immediate family would soon end. I guess my lack of sleep and the rigors of travel had scrambled some of my clear thinking.

It was early evening when I got home, and my grandmother wanted to know if I was hungry. I told her that I was starving. She said we can make you something, or get some restaurant food? I said that I would love to have a Pizza Hut pizza, as it had been two years since I had anything like that. Then my Dad surprised me with a Royal Crown Cola! (RC was nowhere in Vietnam.)

She ordered a large pizza, and I assured her that I would eat the whole thing. When it arrived, I could only eat one slice, as my stomach had shrunk considerably. My weight was 127 pounds when I mustered out. I went to Vietnam well built, full of muscle, and scaled out at 168 pounds.

Once I was home and looked in the mirror, I found myself as a very suntanned and gaunt young man. And I was noticeably thin since I had lost 41 pounds over there. I finally found sleep later that evening, and did not wake up until sometime in the afternoon the following day.

A CHANGED BODY

Living in a totally different environment and country for any given period of time can and will change one's physical makeup. I did come home from Vietnam with several changes within my body's chemistry and makeup. Things were truly different before that climate modified me.

First off, the Malaria pill was always taken on a Monday. It was a large pill, big enough for a horse, and it was very powerful with its side effects.

The Malaria pill basically plugged you up for almost another week, or until you took the next pill. Most of the time, I had the effect of having no bowel movement until the following Monday. Unless I ate a spaghetti meal. Then my system kicked into high gear.

The medics said that everyone responds differently. They went on to say that I was perfectly healthy and normal otherwise, and not to worry about it. My system was just fine according to them. So I just accepted that this was going to be my lifestyle while in country.

My system was haywire for a good year after I came home. Seemed like any type of solid food would plug me up, until I ate something greasy. Then the bomb bay doors fully opened.

Today, I still have numerous side effects from this way of life. I have spoken with several other Vietnam Vets who said that they have experienced and are still experiencing intermittent and irregular bowel movements.

Some have had surgery on their intestines and digestive tract to assist their overall health. I use a probiotic and an OTC polyethylene oral powder to assist me with movement, and I can always use some extra good luck.

The other serious change is my adjustment to the atmospheric temperature on my body.

Living in a daily environment of 100 plus degrees really changed me. I can tolerate hot, humid, and wet weather well. But I cannot handle temperatures below 80 degrees, and any type of bitter cold weather conditions.

Any type of cold weather affects my extremities and breathing. I cannot make my hands and feet stay warm if they get cold. Short of soaking them in a basin of warm to hot water is the only trick to restore the feeling. And the relief never lasts that long. The cold returns quickly.

And these extremities get blueish and white, just like the manner in which frostbite attacks one's health status.

When the weather is getting close to the freezing zone, then that's the time that I also start having breathing challenges. Seems like every inhalation of cold air feels like ice needles ravaging my throat and upper windpipe area.

There have been times when my lungs felt like several scoops of ice entered my lung cavities, and there is a sharp pain associated with all of this.

Even wearing several layers of clothing does not help. Thus, I monitor the weather in the winter time of the year, and try to stay in the warmest possible environment at all times.

RETURN TO CHURCH

The Sunday coming up right after my return home, was to be special for us. My family was scheduled to bring up Holy Communion at the Sunday nine o'clock Mass.

I have served as the church organist ever since fourth grade, and Dad was the head usher. Mom sang in the choir and was a soloist for several special hymns. All of my family was connected to the church in a special way. We contributed our talents to the success of the Church, honoring God, as devoted Faith-bearing Christians and Byzantine Catholics.

The parish priests spoke with my Dad earlier, to ensure that this honored event was to be a part of the overall welcome home for me. They also mentioned to my Dad and Mom that they hoped I would be back playing the organ for the Masses and the choir. With lots of hard work and practice, I completed my credentials as a cathedral organist before high school graduation. So the priests had the utmost respect for my musical talents and qualifications. They counted on me.

I wore my military Class "A" uniform with my Army Firefighter badge proudly hanging beneath my ribbons per the dress standard. I felt that things would be great, and that I would see many of my friends after Mass that Sunday. Not so.

After Mass ended, only one family came up to me to say "Welcome home", and that was a doctor and his wife. This family had their only daughter serving in the Navy, and knew the true sacrifice of serving one's country.

No one else came over. I didn't know if folks were scared of me or that the hatred of the war directed towards active duty personnel drove them to their decision to not speak to me.

I was saddened and deeply affected as I exited the church that morning.

My mind was starting to unravel at this time. I felt that the church was not the same as when I left, and that the congregation was against me. I could not believe that this had just occurred, especially to me. After all, I was well known and served as their primary and principal organist for many years, especially for their families' funerals and weddings. I was the "go-to" musician.

I started to get furious right afterwards, and a flashback of the way I was treated on high school graduation night kicked my bitter memories into high gear. That particular event came back into clear view for me. No forgiveness or present day compensation will ever make this wrong right.

As the youthful church organist I played all of the Masses and other ceremonies and events that no one else wanted to cover during these years. I performed music for all of the daily 5:30 a.m. Masses, including the funerals and Holy Days. This included doing the daily 4:30 a.m. Mass for the Nuns at their convent.

Despite bad weather and extra hours of commitment, I never faltered in these activities. I walked six long city blocks one way to accomplish all of this in every condition of weather, and never took a sick day during four years of high school. I did not do it for any money. I gave of my talent to the church. Once in a great while I would get an honorarium for a wedding.

There were two music teachers/directors for the church and high school at that time. Both were Catholic Nuns, and the younger one fully supported me and gave me excellent direction towards

becoming a true professional. The senior Nun was truly jealous of my talents because I could outperform her and her "pets" in the music class or whenever I played the organ.

She also hated me for the fact that I was the leader and organist/vocalist of a very successful Rock'n'Roll band during my high school time, and enjoyed immense popularity. Soon she discovered, through her pets reporting on me, that I also dated the Protestant girls, whom I met through the dances that the band performed at. Of course that was a big "no-no" back then.

Well on graduation night all of my classmates just figured that the music award was going to me for everything that I did for the church and the school throughout the years.

The announcement was made, and the senior Nun's pet got the award. I could not believe the news when it was announced, and neither did the bulk of my classmates believe it.

My nickname was "Kookie" back then, and everyone close by asked the same question to me... "Kookie, what happened?" "This is your award." "This is bullshit." These were some of the comments that came from my classmates. They were as stunned as I was.

My Mother was burning mad, and went the following day to confront the Nun. Nothing was fixed, and both my Mom and Grandmother stopped all of their charity work for the church, the school, and the Nuns as a result.

All of the ushers told my Dad that it was a real shame. They said many kind things about me and my talent to my Dad, and hoped that I would not quit my good works as the organist for the church choir despite being treated unfairly.

Most of Dad's ushers were WWII and Korean War veterans themselves, and his good buddies overall. In the following weeks after coming home from Vietnam, I would meet some of them at one of the local veteran service clubs, and they bought me many rounds of drinks, as a sign of their appreciation for my Vietnam War service and to welcome me home as a Brother Veteran. They were all glad that I came home safely. In return, I was delighted to be one of them now!

The following week I went to choir practice, and things were better. The choir members warmly welcomed me, and were truly happy that I was home. They delighted in the fact that I was going to be their organist once again.

Several ladies had tears in their eyes when they saw me. They were very sincere in their "welcome home" remarks to me. I could tell by the way they smiled at me, and I received many unexpected hugs.

A PRIVATE PARTY AND THE NEW MUSIC SCENE

About two weeks passed since I came home, and I got a phone call from one of my long time class mates. He had been a roadie for my rock band, the Union Jacks, and wanted to throw a party for me. I said that it would be great, and on that following Saturday evening it would held at his parents' home in their basement.

He pretty much had the basement all full of rock and roll decorations with a nice stereo system.

The "Hippie" culture was in full swing, and I enjoyed the "Mod" look, Lava lamps, and the Blacklight lighting effects on the displayed wall posters.

There were oversize pillows, sofas, and tapestry type rugs that harmonized with the overall theme of things. The paisley design was prevalent throughout the decorated basement.

I was able to be exposed to some really cool music of that era also. Music that I did not get to hear in Vietnam via the armed Forces radio network.

He had albums of Hendrix, Deep Purple, and a wide selection of new and unheard of musicians to play for me, and I thoroughly enjoyed all of the new sounds and songs. I felt anxious to go downtown as soon as possible and purchase some new music for myself.

A number of my former classmates came and were glad that I was home. There was plenty of beer, and I started to finally feel good about being home.

The sole downside to this party was the fact that I was the only male there without a girlfriend.

After being in country about three months I received a "Dear John" letter. My girlfriend said that her mom directed her to break our relationship, as it was going to be too long for her to wait until I got home.

In looking back, I found out that numerous other soldiers received similar letters when they were there in country. It seems like to me that the negative mood about the war was responsible for these types of break-ups. Just an upsetting part of one's life serving your country in Vietnam.

During the party some of the discussion centered around me starting up a band again. My friends all felt that I needed to assemble another band, that would be as good as or better than the Union Jacks, and that I would reach fame and fortune.

I did not start a new band for several months, but instead went on the road for Artists Corporation of America (ACA) as a solo act, and enjoyed a few months of touring and playing music for their clubs. During this short nightclub stint, I met many people who found out that I was a Vietnam Veteran, and they said that they were proud of me for not going to Canada.

About three months passed after I started with ACA, and the Civil Service Board told me that my fire department position was available, and I quit the road, returning to the fire service.

I was assigned to the Hook & Ladder Truck as a Tillerman (steered the rear end), and was one of the first EMT's for the ambulance, as each platoon was detailed one EMT for this position. I have to note that serving as a Tillerman was the best job in the department! I got lucky!!!

My stateside fire career was just starting to kick itself into high gear, thanks to my wartime experience and service with the Army. I was very proud, and grateful for the opportunity.

At this time of my young life, I had no idea that the severe fire duty that I experienced in a war zone would pay off massive dividends in my future career as a firefighter and a chief officer. I truly had a "jump-start" that would be of immeasurable value.

DISLIKE AND DISRESPECT FOR THE VIETNAM VETERAN

There were times when I found myself in a no-win situation when it came to employment opportunities once back home. And some of this was within city governments.

First off I had my heart set on becoming a Chicago Fireman. I wanted to serve on one of the fireboats or a hook & ladder company. So a trip to Chicago City Hall was a priority for this young veteran.

When I got to Chicago I went inside the huge City Hall edifice in the Loop and went directly to the employment office. I spoke with a lady staffer about needing an application for the Chicago Fire Department (CFD). As she was pulling the paperwork, she asked for my driver's license, which I quickly presented it to her. It was issued in Iowa.

She said "do I have an Illinois license for identification?" I said "no, as I had just returned from serving with the Army in Vietnam."

She then asked for any mail that was delivered to me at my Chicago Illinois address for the past three years. I told her again that I was in the Army in Vietnam, and never lived in Chicago. I just wanted to join the fire department.

She said that I could not get an application since I had not been a Chicago resident for at least three years. I could not believe what I was hearing.

I told her that I should have Veterans Preference, but she said that without the three year Chicago residency requirement being met, that I could not receive an application. So my heart was broken and I returned home.

Several years ago I mentioned this encounter to a retired CFD chief, who was about five years older than me, and he said that to the best of his knowledge, he had never heard of a residency requirement. He thought that this staffer just didn't like Vietnam Vets, and that she "scored one for the team" in turning me away.

The retired chief said that the mood of the City of Chicago was combative to the war, and even unkind to the local Vietnam Vets during that timeframe. He regretted that I experienced such an incident. He and I have remained steadfast fire service colleagues.

In fact throughout the years, I have made many friends in the CFD, and I was permitted to ride along with several "elite" companies, like Snorkel Squad 1 (SS1), thereby gaining skills that could never have been taught in any fire academy. I was most fortunate once again!

THE OLD COLLEGE TRY

The anti-war sentiment was paramount everywhere in our country when I came home. And that included the local community college. I was in for a shock, to say the least, when I walked through the doors.

At the end of May 1972 I went to the Registrar's office to sign up for the summer session. I had about a year and a half of hours built up and figured that I would try for completion of my Associate Degree. That way I would have something towards a higher degree, and I felt that music would be it, since fire science degrees were several years away.

The only other option was to go to Oklahoma State University that offered a fire engineering degree for four years. That avenue would have made me a fire systems graduate, which would have taken me to design fire protection systems and sprinklers. That just wasn't me…I had to have action!

After I signed up, I went into the hallways to see what changes occurred since I left there in 1968. Then I headed towards the student lounge, got a Coke, and sat down hoping to encounter someone I knew. No such luck.

In fact, no one came to my table. Several young people looked at me, and then glanced around the room, going to another table, and some were crowded.

What I finally realized was that I did not look like them. I was clean-cut, dressed in normal clothes, and still had a deep tan. The "Hippie" look was in full display here. I got the message real quick.

After consuming the Coke, I started having an uneasy feeling, and saw people glance at me and look quickly away, like I didn't notice their actions. Then the thought that I was not welcome at the college hit me upside my head. I also figured that I would probably be resented by the college staff, and would be treated with bad grades. I figured that Vietnam Vets were the social outcasts here.

I also said to myself that these young kids probably heard of the Union Jacks, but now that I went off to war, I would be treated and looked upon quite differently.

I assume that I was there about 45 minutes or so, and no one came my way. In fact, it appeared that they went out of their way to avoid me.

My young mind started shifting into overdrive, and I knew right then to forget about being a student, either part-time or full-time.

I got up and went back to the Registrar's office, and said that I changed my mind about attending college right now. I asked for a cancellation and got my tuition back without one question being asked.

It was the mid-1980's before I started working on my degrees and that was done and completed with distance learning. I just found out that hard feelings towards war vets were going to be around for a long time, especially in the colleges.

THE HOMETOWN BLOW

The biggest shock in employment discrimination came to me when I applied for the fire chief's position in my home town, where I was born. (BTW...I am a WWII Marine brat.) I was then currently the fire chief in Moss Bluff, Louisiana, and wanted to try my luck where I was born.

The outgoing fire chief suffered a coronary on the job, forcing his medical retirement immediately. He was an absolute gentleman, and a next-door neighbor and good friend of mine.

I must report that I served as his fire chaplain for his funeral recently. He and I ran into each other when I was in Iowa, having just finished playing music at the annual memorial service for the firefighters. He told me that he would be deeply honored for me to be his selectee as chaplain for his Final Honors. I said "sure, it will be a sincere honor for me" and that "I will see you in about twenty years". He must have known that his time was near.

I might add that he was quite an excellent carpenter. In fact, he helped me make a professional extension speaker cabinet for use in my keyboard position with the Union Jacks band in my late high school years. No one could tell that it was not factory made.

Anyway, I went through the whole application process and did quite well. I was the only combat veteran that applied for the vacancy. There was another Vietnam vet who applied and qualified, but he was in the arms room, and served in a support position while he was in country. No combat duties were incurred, nor was he a military firefighter in any capacity.

I came certified in many disciplines, with an extensive background in military, civilian, industrial, and volunteer departments as the chief, and was completing my master's degree in fire science. I also just finished apprentice time with the world renowned "Boots & Coots" Wild Well Firefighters, and became a life-long colleague of Dwight Williams, of Williams Fire & Hazard Control, through a major incident that occurred at the Strategic Petroleum Reserve.

In addition to my military leadership, I had already served as the fire chief for two of our country's largest major chemical and petro-chemical installations and complexes, plus built an excellent volunteer-to-combination fire department from the ground up.

The test for the position was the highly respected David Gratz based assay from the University of Maryland Fire Institute program. It was tough, but very thorough. I felt that I did well, but I never received my score after I took it. In fact, I never heard back from the city about anything related to the test score. I only received a letter for my appointment time and date for the verbal interview portion after the written test.

When I went to the verbal interview process, and sat among the other candidates, I noticed that I was the only one truly prepared for this stage of the process. Everyone else walked in the interview room with empty hands.

I came with four dossiers full of pertinent information about my career, copies of certificates and commendations, my military records, training, and even a current professional studio color photo of myself in my Chief's Class "A" uniform. All of this was bound in a very nice, bright red, presentation folder, and they were handed off to each member of the three man panel.

I was the last of the candidates to be interviewed, and so the atmosphere appeared to be more relaxed with the panel. They were not watching the clock at this point. I truly believed that they were impressed, as they wanted to hear "war stories" about my work with the Wild Well control specialists, and the large chemical plants.

They also asked about how my time was in Louisiana, especially with the culture, food, and music. They already knew that I was a professional musician, and very popular in the local area, both as a solo artist and as a band leader. The verbal interview actually ended on a high note.

Several months later I came upon one of the panel members at the local Walgreens after church on a Sunday afternoon. He said it was good to see me, and said he felt disappointed about me not being selected. He said that I received the highest rating from the panel, which he further stated was the highest score received by any of the candidates.

A non-veteran was chosen, much to the overall chagrin of the department's membership. I did offer him congratulations when I met him later on the street. I felt that I must have scored poorly on the exam, and I got disqualified by that measure. Wow! I was wrong...

About a year passed and I was back up in Iowa again to perform firefighter and patriotic music at the annual memorial ceremony. I bumped into one of the assistant chiefs, who was also a finalist candidate for the position, at a local grocery store, and we enjoyed a great visit. Then he turned our conversation to the fire chief selection process.

This assistant chief told me that everyone felt that I had the job "in-the-bag". I looked at him in disbelief, and said I never heard anything more after the selection process. I also told him that I always wondered why I never even received a thank you note from the city administration, which was an accepted practice for recognizing high level position candidates for their efforts.

He told me that I scored the highest on the test. He went on to say in fact, that nationwide no one wrote a higher test score than I did at that time. I was shocked and asked him what did I score? He said that I wrote a 147 out of a possible 150 points. He also said that no one broke above a 90, and that the selectee reportedly scored a 70 overall according to the rumor mill.

He did say that the mayor was against me because I was a Vietnam Vet, and this mayor hated anyone associated with the war. It was discrimination for sure. Wish the laws that protect us now were in force back then.

After two other civilian job actions went sour for basically the same reasons, I applied for Federal Civil Service, and soon discovered that this is where I should have been all along since my discharge.

The Veterans Readjustment Act (VRA) was in full force at that timeframe of the late 1980's. I applied and was quickly hired for a vacancy at the Savanna Army Depot's Fire Department in northwestern Illinois, and have never looked back at this worthwhile decision.

The fair treatment of veterans is paramount within the Federal Civil Service system. I have made many lifelong and treasured friends through my work within the Federal Civil Service Fire & Emergency Services at numerous military installations worldwide.

The end result here for me was that I got exposed to the hidden side of an unfavorable political climate. I started to understand that the best candidate doesn't get the job. A lot of incompetent and small-minded people in city management are threatened by strong, driven, and dedicated personnel. Vietnam Vets don't have time for these types of games and people.

A PREPARATION FOR LIFE AND CAREER

As I can now look back, I value everything from my life as an Army Soldier-Firefighter in Vietnam, and the tough times paid the largest dividends.

I experienced challenges that would probably have never come across my life, should I have lived my life as a regular civilian firefighter.

At the darkest of times, we were caught between two distinct enemies, one being "Old-Man-Fire" and a determined communist army, who really wanted us either dead or gone.

All of the unknown factors taught me to constantly "adjust fire" to meet the enemy and related threats. I must say that I gained tremendous experience that could not have been taught, much less learned, in any type of stateside position.

The environment of a war zone constantly evolves, and one must pay attention 100% of the time to witness the ongoing movement. By remaining alert, applying courage, and making common sense decisions, got me home in one piece.

I truly feel that my military background gave me a superior advantage, which I still use to this day, in meeting all the numerous challenges in my life and career as a firefighter.

In the military, combat veterans know how to "adjust fire" and adapt to about anything. I was lucky to be that type of student!

PRAYERS ALL THE TIME

I was raised in both the Byzantine and Roman Catholic faith. My parents and grandparents saw that I was brought up in the best possible manner. I am forever grateful to them and for what they did and sacrificed for me. I have been uniquely blessed with my Faith in God.

I said prayers constantly while I was in Vietnam. If I told you that I have prayed thirty times on any given day during my time there, then it was true.

Back then, the chapels and churches were full of soldiers at every service. I played music for countless Catholic services and also many Protestant services during my stateside time, before my orders came for Vietnam. There was no shame to be a Christian Soldier.

When I got my orders for Vietnam I did not feel that I was ever coming home, except in a pine box with Old Glory covering my remains.

In advance preparation of my uncertain future, I even had the small treasures of my life all cleaned up and neatly stored in cardboard boxes on the basement shelves before I left for Vietnam.

My possessions were my deeply treasured childhood model fire engines and my Lionel trains.

The music equipment, from my "Union Jacks" band time, was stacked against the north side basement wall. It really hurt to look at them one last time as I performed these storage functions.

My Saint Florian confirmation medal went with me to Vietnam and stayed around my neck with the dog-tags. A special prayer card was kept in my wallet the whole time I was in country. This prayer card is still with me, just like Saint Florian's medal is, on my daily journey through life.

The prayer was given by the Pope to Emperor Charles when he was going into battle in 1505 during the Crusades. It was written in 50 AD and is ordinarily known in the Catholic Church as the "Prayer to Saint Joseph".

The Church issued this proclamation about this prayer for anyone going into battle, or harm's way.

"Whoever shall read this prayer or hear it, or keep it about themselves, shall never die a sudden death or be drowned, nor shall poison take effect on them; neither shall they fall into the hands of the enemy, or shall be burned in any fire or shall be overpowered in battle."

I believe!

A SHADOW OF SHAME

For many years after being home, I never spoke about my military time and/or service with the Army in Vietnam. I felt it best to keep it quiet, even in the employment circles.

I wanted to be comfortable in society and treated kindly. The newspaper accounts scared all of us. We felt that there was another war environment here in America that we now had to face as returning Vietnam Veterans. Life was uncomfortable at times. Did we have any friends outside of the AMVETS, VFW, and American Legion organizations?

This was not a "respected" war, like WWII or Korea. I even kept my military medals and fire service memorabilia in unmarked boxes at home in storage. I felt a sense of blame for things, since America did not "win" the war, even though I served as a firefighter and received an Honorable Discharge. Firefighters were supposed to be one of the "good" guys.

When I went out on dates, I never brought up the subject of being a Vietnam Veteran, much less a veteran, as I did not want my date to break things off with me. I wanted to love and be loved again.

Some of my war scars from my injuries were initially ugly and visible on my face. Fortunately they have faded or blended in over time, and are not very noticeable now, unless pointed out. But a few of the girls that I dated after I got home, did notice them, and asked me what happened.

Surprisingly all of my girlfriends were kind to me, and said they were sorry that bad things happened to me. Several even told me that they were proud of me because I wasn't a "draft-dodger"! It was nice to hear that, but little comfort came overall.

THE VA AND ME

I had been home about six months or so, and I then went to the VA to file a claim, not for money, but for the purpose of ensuring that medical care would be rendered to me should I have a medical or skin condition appear later on.

I was awarded a 0% disability for the scars and tissue damage. The medical doctor who saw me, was always checking his watch during our time together. I felt that this was a waste of his time and mine, and I never returned to the VA for anything for over four decades, except for the testing of the Agent Orange exposure, and being placed on the official register.

I never mentioned to the VA during my initial workup about all the inhalation injuries that I suffered during my firefighter duty time. Like I wrote about earlier, it was just "part of the job" being a Smoke-Eater or "old-school fireman".

Another fear that I had from my initial VA encounter was the fact that I did not want a "Disabled Veteran" tag hung on me. I thought that it would jeopardize my career and promotional opportunities. So I kept these things to myself for well over forty-five plus years.

It's only been the last couple of years that Brother Vietnam vets started talking to me about coming to their group sessions and meetings, and convincing me that I need to re-establish my connection with the VA for help. This turned out to be a good thing.

I am forever grateful to them, and I am very comfortable interfacing with the VA now. In fact, all of the VA medical staff and personnel that I have required assistance from, have been very professional and caring, and prompt in their service to my requests for attention and care!

These Brother Vets have made a big difference in my life and career history about being a veteran and serving my country.

I am solid and confident in my Army service for my country, and this memoir is my testament.

I must mention at this time, which is near the end of my writing, is the fact that the VA staff who oversee the awarding of a disability is becoming a great concern to me. I won't go into detail here, but I trust and hope that a fair decision will be coming my way towards my disability.

There are reasons for my concerns here as there was such a limited number of firefighters in the Army in Vietnam, and no one gave us any thought back then unless you needed us. I believe that the VA doesn't know what to do with when we ask for any type of disability compensation.

I hope they give me a fair shake and other deserving veteran firefighters.

MARRIAGE, A MISCARRIAGE, AND LOVE ON THE ROCKS

I came home changed, although I did not know it for some time. As I presently look back, it's easy to see now. Sure thought that I was always the same person with the same lifestyle and mannerisms after the war.

In my high school years I enjoyed being the organist and leader of the "Union Jacks" band in the Midwest. The band was extremely popular and well known throughout the Midwestern states.

We were signed on with the Morris Agency of Chicago, and had a "Top 40" hit record of that timeframe's 45 rpm standard. Despite being in the remaining years of our high school education, we were doing mini-touring and lots of shows during our free time.

The Morris Agency also had REO Speedwagon signed on at the same time as they had the Union Jacks. The Morris staff quickly found out to not book both bands anywhere close to each other. The reason being was that the Union Jacks outdrew REO. We had quite a show.

There would be about a thousand kids at our dances, and maybe a couple hundred at REO's dances. I have always wondered what would have happened to us if the bassist and I did not have forthcoming draft numbers. The Union Jacks could have probably made the big time.

The band was full of good looking guys and we all had lots of girlfriends, to say the least.

I met a slender and very attractive brunette on the band's break during a performance one weekend. She was three years behind me in school, and just kept staring me down the whole time I was on stage. But then again, this was pretty much how it was back then in the 1960's. Girls loved the boys-in-the-band. And we loved them back!

She told all her lady friends that she was going to marry the Union Jacks' organist as soon as she graduated. Her friends all gave her the razz, and said "good luck" and "dream on"!

Of course, I disappeared into the Army and went off to Vietnam. She never crossed my mind until I was home and saw her as the cashier supervisor at the local K-Mart. Wow!

My grandmother asked if I could take her to K-Mart to help her pick up some bulky items that day, and it was fortunate timing for me. I might not have ran into my future bride otherwise.

We visited for a while there in the store, and then I asked her for a date when she was free. Of course it was that evening, and away we went. A fairytale romance that shifted into high gear.

I was on the fire department with steady employment, and soon we were making wedding plans. We could not have been any happier. In fact we were so happy together, that she had me re-write our marriage vows to say "For Time and Eternity" instead of "til Death do us part".

Our folks and friends were all happy for us too. We got married in September 1972, and then we moved to Louisiana in January of 1976 for better employment opportunities.

I had a great job offer at the very young age of 26, and became the paid industrial fire chief at the world renown and very huge OLIN Chemicals Complex in Lake Charles, Louisiana. My salary more than doubled when they discussed my hiring benefits. I could hardly believe what good fortune had come my way.

We bought our new home shortly afterwards in Moss Bluff, and soon thereafter I was selected as the first volunteer chief of the newly formed Ward 1 Fire Protection District. I became a "dual-hatted" fire chief, with two departments to manage and supervise.

I was basically working day and night trying to make everything go right for both fire departments.

Everything was extremely serious to me, and I never took time to relax with her and have some type of different fun. I figured that we were both having fun with all the firefighting activities.

It was basically what I did in Vietnam. Everything was serious and I never relaxed, nor did I want to, as I felt that I was going about things correctly.

We never had a vacation. Our honeymoon was it. In looking back, I was more married to my career, then her. Finally things melted down at a timeline of seven years.

She left the marriage, and we had an uncontested parting. Nothing ugly occurred after our separation, as she went off to find her happiness, and I buried myself in my career to stay sane.

Looking back with 20/20 hindsight, I can see where the war's environment changed me. My time in Vietnam was the time that I needed to grow and learn how to love in a safe setting with young women my age.

Instead I learned how to fight fire and the communists, thereby scarring my memory and doing nothing for my growth in loving a woman. I feel that many of us got cheated out of this part of our lives. We were fighting and not learning about loving. It's that simple.

Upon coming home, I did not truly know how to love, or even attempt it. I thought that having sex was all you needed for love.

Fortunately I never hit her, nor was I mean or abusive to her during our time together. She had a new beautiful home, a new Mustang automobile, and great clothes. She didn't have me.

Several years ago she came to one of my musical concerts. She came up to the stage afterwards, while I was tearing down, and surprised me. She looked fantastic and we had a great visit.

Overall, it was surreal to me. The sad part was that I did not have a husband's love or feelings toward her, and I even felt bewildered that she used to be my wife.

She told me that she still loves me, but not as a wife, just as a very special person in her life.

Every now and then, something will happen to remind me of her. I must mention that she was a look-alike copy of Cher, except more beautiful. Long hair, slender, and very kind and polite to all who came in contact with her.

Thus, when I see old re-runs of Sonny & Cher, I immediately think of her. I get sad and depressed when these occasions occur. I truly feel that the conditions of war in the distant land of Vietnam changed me forever.

I must also mention that we did not have children together. Around the timeframe of 1974, which was about two years into our marriage, I started to receive several mailed documents, questionnaires, and form-type letters. All of these concerns centered around the military's use of the Agent Orange herbicide, and the overall chemical atmosphere question of serving in Vietnam. It was downright scary to receive these publications!

What I started to learn and understand was that the hidden nature of these war chemicals were of great concern to countless numbers of veterans, who were becoming afflicted with immediate and very strange health conditions. It shocked me as I read more and more published literature.

Our nation's medical community was starting to take a serious look at what was causing such a wide variety of unexplainable medical maladies.

Despite this being pre-Internet days, there was plenty of written activity in, with, and through the various hard copy correspondence to discover what was going on to our in-country veterans.

I had a buddy that served as an artilleryman and was sprayed from an airborne drop of Agent Orange. He told me that the whole gun crew was soaked from the passing aircraft.

After coming home and resuming his lifestyle, he and his wife had twins about a year later.

Unfortunately, both of the children suffered birth defects, despite her carrying her term with no health issues. There were no indications that the pregnancy would be of concern.

Prior to his service time, they had one child, and the young male was very healthy, growing up without any health issues or concerns.

He and his wife were very healthy, physically fit, and strong individuals. Nothing could be found by their doctors in their health profiles and history that would give credence as to why their children were born with these negative results.

After I visited with him and his wife, and saw the kids, I felt that there was cause for alarm.

I knew that our chemical based fires were always a tough challenge for us, and when we "ate smoke" from these blazes, we were truly sick. Looking back at these fires, I feel that maybe some type of chemical deposit is being carried in either our blood or skin tissue, and awaiting an unknown moment to surface and wreak havoc upon our overall health.

My ex and I had several discussions about having children, and decided to not have any since the growing evidence was starting to scream loudly about my war chemical exposure in Vietnam.

Way too much would be at stake. I was also privately concerned that my seed could somehow poison her, and I did not want to lose her. I never shared this thought with her.

We felt that since we were young, we could wait it out until we knew more about the whole situation. I truly regret not having children with her. It's a sad part of my life.

I have heard that war cheats you out of life, and I have to say that I agree with this statement, whereas there is time that can never be recovered. Treasured moments are forever lost.

Now with 47 years of separation with my ex-wife, I have been told by her of a most unfortunate event that occurred early into our marriage. She kept this to herself all these years.

She and I re-connected during a couple of occasions during this past year. We stayed in a manner of irregular touch, and kept out of each other's business, unless something required us to converse with each other.

Fortunately for me, she is a retired nurse with an extensive background in many disciplines of the medical field. I recently injured myself, resulting in a severe hernia, when lifting a heavy musical instrument keyboard. Thus, I had to face a serious hernia surgery, and I asked her to help me during my recovery time as a personal nurse. She politely agreed to assist.

When I got home after the surgery, a few days passed by, and then she asked me to share a visit, as she wanted my undivided attention. I agreed and made time for her to dialogue with me.

She said that she suffered a miscarriage when I was away on duty-time attending an EMT seminar out of town for a week. The timeframe was a little over a year into our marriage.

It was the start of her third trimester, and everything happened rapidly. She passed the fetus, and did not suffer during the event, nor have any negative life-threatening results.

She said that she did not want to tell me because she was scared and afraid. She felt that it would have hurt me to know, and she didn't know that she was pregnant herself. She said that she was too confused at the young age of twenty to even understand what occurred.

Of course I am hurt, and upon hearing the news left me numb and without a sense of reason. I feel badly for her, as I never wanted any harm to ever come to her, and hope that to this day she's not haunted by such a tragic event. I, of course, am still coming to grips on this. I re-visit this daily, and am saddened that the loss of a child is forever, at least in our mortal world.

I must press on with my Faith, and know that a handsome son is awaiting me in Heaven.

I have to go back to what I firmly believe is that these various war chemicals are the root cause of countless maladies of the Vietnam veteran.

While Agent Orange is our most visible and silent enemy, there were other chemicals unleashed upon us too. With the lack of breathing protection for the soldier-firefighters, there is no question that we inhaled and were easily exposed to the raw effects of such potent mixtures during the hazardous work of the MOS while in Vietnam.

It's a shame that the Veterans Affairs authorities continue to deny the presence of such wide-spread afflictions, and ignore and deny claims.

The handful of soldier-firefighters, who served in Vietnam, is but a minute number. Due recognition will never be forthcoming in our MOS now, much less our lifetime. Maybe after we're all dead, someone in the VA will realize the tragic oversight. That's way too late!

To me, it's never too late to right a wrong!

CHIEF PETERSEN'S INSPIRATION

I must make mention of the positive role model that Chief Petersen was to me. He was clever and innovative in whatever he took to task.

Well before the coined phrase of "thinking outside of the box" became vogue, he was doing it!

He would search for abandoned military equipment and hardware that could be converted into useful and practical firefighting assets. There were times when he would also obtain unusual items that did not have a direct connection to firefighting, but were added to the overall inventory for a future purpose. His stockpile was interesting and eclectic, to say the least.

When the time would come, Chief Petersen would then use these stockpiled items to swap for other pieces of equipment. He then went on to create and construct another item of value for the success of the fire department.

His skills in reworking and rebuilding unwanted scrap material into professional hardware was truly inspirational to a young man like myself.

During my pre-teen and teenage years, I was a champion model car builder, and won many contests. Thus, I could directly relate to his methods and ways of doing business. His talents inspired me then, and have continued to inspire me throughout my entire life.

I cannot imagine my life without his positive influence and guiding hand.

A FINAL COMMENT

I would be remiss here if I did not offer a comment about how truly lucky I am. I came home in one piece and have made the best out of things that occurred to me from Vietnam. One only has to look around and see that many Blessings have been bestowed upon me and my life.

There are times when I wonder "what if" and then I try to let it all be memories, as that's what each individual must do to keep moving forward in life.

I am saddened that one of my high school buddies, who was mustered in with me, was KIA. And that several of my military service friends have died an early death, which was war related.

We cannot erase this period of time in our country's history. Nor can we forget.

Courage and understanding must be applied to assist and help us realize that our lives are not perfect, even in service to God and Country.

I have a treasure chest full of true friends who respect and love me for serving. Many are non-veterans. They have welcomed me unconditionally as a Vietnam Veteran.

They keep me as a part of their daily lives. How can one describe this genuine inclusion?

I am Blessed!

RETROSPECT

I stand proud of my U. S. Army service time in Vietnam, and felt that I contributed in a positive way to the overall war effort.

I truly feel that the Soldier-Firefighters of Long Binh performed many duties and services to protect our nation's soldiers and assets in a remote part of the world in the highest traditions of the United States Army with great courage and dedication to duty.

I salute my Brother Firefighters in Fatigues!

AN ARMY FIREFIGHTER IN VIETNAM 1970-1971

U.S. ARMY DA-1 FIRE REPORT

FIRE DEPARTMENT INDIVIDUAL RUN REPORT		POST
The proponent agency for this form is Office Chief of Engineers.		Fire Department, Long Binh

TYPE OF TRUCK	REGISTRY NO.	STATION NO.	DATE
2½ Ton 6x6 Class 530B	4H 3588	Fire Station #1	25 October 1970

ALARM DATA		TIME RESPONDED	
RECEIVED FROM ☐ Box No. ☒ Phone ☐ Other	TO FIRE A.M. 2010 P.M.	TO COVER—IN A.M. 2011 P.M.	

TIME RETURNED TO STATION	TOTAL TIME OUT	MILEAGE		
A.M. P.M. 2020	HOURS 0	MINUTES 10	IN 6711 OUT 6710	TRAVELED 1

LOCATION OF FIRE OR ORIGIN OF ALARM
CPO Gate - Intersection of Outer Ring Road and Hawaii Street

DESCRIPTION OF PROPERTY INVOLVED
Grass Fire

CLASSIFICATION OF ALARM

FIRE	NO FIRE
☐ In Building ☒ In Brush, Grass, Rubbish, etc.	☐ Rescue or Emergency ☐ Accidental Alarm
☐ In Vehicle ☐ In Brush, Grass, Rubbish near Bldg.	☐ Plane Crash (Standby) ☐ Other (Specify)
☐ In Airplane ☐ Other (Specify)	☐ False Alarm

EQUIPMENT USED OR CONSUMED

NUMBER	AMOUNT	ITEM	NUMBER	AMOUNT	ITEM
	Unit	2½-gallon Soda-Acid	1	Lines	Booster Hose
	Unit	2½-gallon Foam		Ft.	1½-inch Hose
	Unit	2½-gallon Pump Tank		Ft.	2½-inch Hose
	Unit	5-gallon Pump Tank		Ft.	Ladders
	Unit	15-pound Carbon Dioxide		Lb.	Foam Powder
	Unit	50-pound Carbon Dioxide		Gal.	Foam Solution
	Gal.	Carbon Tetrachloride		Lb.	Calcium Chloride (Nonfreeze)
	Unit	40-gallon Soda-Acid			(Other)
	Unit	40-gallon Foam			(Other)
		(Other)			(Other)

HOSE LINE

		FT. LINE	INCH HOSE	INCH NOZZLE	HOUR	MINUTE
Line 1	Hydrant					
	Pumper					
	Booster	150	1	1	0	5
Line 2	Hydrant					
	Pumper					
	Booster					
Line 3	Hydrant					
	Pumper					
	Booster					

WORKING TIME OF PUMPER			ESTIMATED QUANTITY WATER USED			
HOURS	MINUTES	GALLONS	HYDRANT	PUMPER	BOOSTER	
0	6	80	0	80	80	

DA FORM 5-1, 1 DEC 44 This form supersedes WD AGO Form 5-1, 4 September 1944, (Old WD AGO Form 412) which may be used until existing stocks are exhausted.

MICHAEL LOUIS KUK

U.S. ARMY DA-1 FIRE REPORT

EQUIPMENT DAMAGED OR DESTROYED

NONE

EQUIPMENT LOST OR FOUND

NONE

PERSONNEL ON DUTY WHEN ALARM RECEIVED

C/C Kuk
D/O Maull
D/O Knott
F/F Browning
C/C Thanh
F/F Thai   F/F Nho

PERSONNEL NOT RESPONDING—REASON

NONE

OFF-DUTY PERSONNEL RESPONDING

NONE

MECHANICAL PERFORMANCE OF VEHICLE

Good

REMARKS (Indicate Accident, Injury, Fatality, Etc.):

NONE

OPERATION OF UNIT AND STORY OF CALL

Give complete essential details as briefly as possible, including sequence of operations, exact location, observations as to origin and progress of fire, untoward happenings, etc. Information of value in final investigation by board of officers is essential. Where appropriate, make sketch showing location of hydrants, pumper, hose lines, and other operations with respect to building, or buildings, involved.

At approximately 2010 hours, 25 October 1970, Sgt Teyto (6992) reported a grass fire at the CPO Gate, intersection of Outer Ring Road and Hawaii Street, by telephone (117). Upon arrival the fire was burning inside the two gates next to the guard shack. The locks were cut on both gates in order to gain entry for extinguishment. Extinguishment was completed with one booster line and 80 gallons of water. Returned to station and back in service at 2020 hours.

SKETCH

NONE

SUBMITTED BY	CLASSIFICATION	DATE
Michael L. Kuk	Crew Chief	25 Oct 1970
CHECKED BY	TITLE (Chief or Assistant Chief)	
Cha Hyong Man	Assistant Chief	

THE CD FROM COMMUNICATIONS

I have a Compact Disc that has approximately fifty-three and a half minutes of audio radio traffic. This brief recording alone tells a story of the intense fire alarm activity and responses of the firefighters to a myriad of alarms on a major holiday.

Since the RTO and the Communications room never get any of the limelight that is always afforded to the firefighters in general, and they were the true initial action team, I took it upon myself to set up a simple cassette recorder in the Alarm Room on New Year's Eve 1970 to capture the robust activity.

Little did I know that this period would be the busiest tour of duty for the LBFD. Twenty one alarms were responded to during this timeframe of twelve hours. We had fourteen fire calls on Christmas Day, and we thought that would be the record!

In listening to the tape recording, one can understand the "Gung-Ho" attitude of the Soldier-Firefighters. Everyone was ready to respond and protect our military installation, despite the uneasiness of being briefed that our enemy might try for an all-out assault during New Years.

We spread out our manpower and used two and three man companies on the engines. The water tenders just had a solo driver. We figured that the base would come under attack, and by having an increase in our fire apparatus, with a reduced crew, then we could respond to several fires at once, and hopefully make a difference by initiating some limited firefighting action. It payed off here for us during this period, as everyone thought that a major assault would be forthcoming.

You'll hear the RTO answering the fire phones and talking on the radio simultaneously, never losing his cool. And you will also hear several firefighters, the 530-B diesels starting up and leaving the station, an occasional siren, and lots of busy radio traffic from the fire units.

There were times when the RTO did not receive any immediate radio response from the rigs. As I mentioned earlier in this writing, portable radios were still being developed, and not assigned to any of the firefighters. (Just the two PA&E chiefs.) Fortunately radios were in the cabs of most of the apparatus. Thus, one had to get back to the engine to report anything of value. Even a brief reply on the truck's console took this action. So a delay was commonplace back then.

This CD is a verifier of what really did happen in the Vietnam War. There was plenty of action when things start occurring. Having military firefighters on duty and at the ready does strongly testify that the protection of our soldiers and military assets are of paramount importance!

If you desire a copy of the CD, then please eMail me at ss1mlk@hotmail.com with your mailing address. I will write you back and advise you of the cost of postage/packaging to ship you this notable recording. The CD is my gift to you.

LEGEND

AC	Air Conditioning
AD	After the Birth of Our Lord
ACA	Artists Corporation of America
AFFF	Aqueous Film Forming Foam
AIT	Advanced Infantry Training or Advanced Individual Training
AMVETS	American Veterans Organization
APC	Armored Personnel Carrier
BN	Battalion
CB	Chlorobromomethane
CD	Compact Disc
CCL4	Carbon Tetrachloride
CFD	Chicago Fire Department
CFR	Crash-Fire-Rescue
Class 1	Ammunition and Ordnance
CO	Commanding Officer
CO2	Carbon Dioxide
COPD	Congestive Obstructive Pulmonary Disease
CPR	Cardio Pulmonary Resuscitation

C-Rations	Military food in a sealed metal can
Cuu Hoa	Firefighter in Vietnamese
DA	Department of the Army
DAV	Disabled American Veteran
DFW	Dallas-Fort Worth Airport Identification Code
DOA	Dead on Arrival
DOD	Department of Defense
EN	Engineers
Engine	Firefighting Pumper
EOD	Explosive Ordnance Disposal
ETS	End of Time Served
EVAC	Evacuation Hospitals (24th or 93rd)
FD	Fire Department
FES	Fire and Emergency Services
FOB	Forward Operating Base
GI	Government Issue or civilian slang for an American Soldier
GPM	Gallon(s) Per Minute
HAM	Amateur radio for non-commercial messaging
Hi-Ex	High Expansion Foam
HVAC	Heating, Ventilation, and Air Conditioning
IV	Intravenous Medical Drug Therapy
KIA	Killed In Action
Kiowa	Small Rotary Wing Aircraft – manufactured by Bell
LBFD	Long Binh Fire Department
LBJ	Long Binh Jail or Long Binh Junction
LDH	Large Diameter Hose
M-14	Fully Automatic American Military Rifle (predecessor to the M-16)
MACV	Military Assistance Command - Vietnam
Medevac	Rotary Wing (Huey) Medical Aircraft
MP	Military Police

MoGas	Regular grade gasoline
MOH	Medal of Honor
MOS	Military Occupational Specialty
MP	Military Police
MPH	Miles per Hour
MSA	Mine Safety Appliances
NCO	Non Commissioned Officer
NCOIC	Non Commissioned Officer in Charge
NPT	National Pipe Thread
NST	National Standard Thread (Fire hose thread)
NVA	North Vietnamese Army
OIC	Officer in Charge
OTC	Over the Counter
PA	Public Address System
PA&E	Pacific Architects and Engineers
PACT	2022 expanded VA coverage legislation
PenePrime	Road Sealing Oil and Coating
POL	Petroleum-Oil-Lube
PPE	Personal Protective Equipment
PTSD	Post Traumatic Stress Disorder
R&R	Rest and Relaxation
RPG	Rocket Propelled Grenade
RPM	Revolutions per Minute
RTO	Radio Telephone Operator
SCBA	Self-Contained Breathing Apparatus
Silvers	Nickname for the Aluminized Crash-Fire-Rescue Protective Clothing
SS1	Snorkel Squad 1 – a highly elite fire-rescue component of the Chicago FD
Tender	Water Tanker truck
USA	United States Army or United States of America
USAF	United States Air Force

USARV	United States Army - Republic of Vietnam
VA	Veterans Administration
VC	Viet Cong
VFW	Veterans of Foreign Wars
VIP	Very Important Person or Party
VRA	Veterans Readjustment Act
WWII	World War II
011A	American LaFrance Airfield Crash Truck
11B	Light Weapons Infantry MOS
51M	Military Firefighter MOS
530-B	Military standard 2-1/2 ton chassis multi-purpose fire engine

PHOTO SECTION

Author in his Army Khaki's at North Fort Polk Fire Station 2. P-750 "Boxcar" engine on the left, and the International structural Class A engine on the right.

Long Binh Station 1 with the primary response apparatus.

Long Binh Station 1 with apparatus at the ready.

View from the Alarm Room, looking out at the apparatus floor.

East side view of Station 1's outside storage of the extra apparatus. Chief's pickup on the left, and the blue water tender on the right.

Left-to-right. Engine 6, Foam 2, the Tank. They were quartered outside under tarps. All-wood Station 1 was built for just four stalls.

Engines 3, 4, 5, on the apron. Rescue 1 inside its stall.

The 1953 Federal. Outside storage. Note the tarps.

Jeep 1 sported amber glass headlights to aid in leading responses in dense fog. Blue tender in the background.

Fire Jeep 1 with the Deluge gun dismounted.

Jeep 1 with the Deluge Gun mounted.

AN ARMY FIREFIGHTER IN VIETNAM 1970-1971

The Tank in its glory with Jeep 1.

The Tank with its raised High-Ex foam applicator boom nozzle.

Ground view of the front of the Tank.

The Tank with Jeeps 1 and 3.

Sitting atop of the business end of the Tank.

Engine 6, Foam 2, and the Tank at the ready. "Tres Amigos!"

Engine 6 with Foam 3. Always outside.

Pump panel of Engine 6. Note the pole-mounted Searchlight.

Rearview of Foam 3 showing the foam delivery piping and hardware.

Foam 3 with its large High-Ex foam nozzle generator on the front bumper.

Standing by Engine 3. Note the European colored blue beacon light.

Getting ready to respond on Engine 3.

Working radio traffic. Good image of the Maltese Cross.

In the Crew Chief's position using the two-way radio.

"Mounting up" to the Crew Chief's seat on Engine 3.

Standing on the tailboard of Engine 3.

Getting ready to respond on Foam 2.

Foam 2 with the Extinguisher shop directly behind.

Relaxed pose in front of Foam 2, with the Tank barely visible on the right.

Just striking another pose in front of Foam 2 and the Tank. (We sometimes took duplicates, as one did not know if one's hand shook during the snapshot.)

Rear and side view of Foam 2.

The "business" side of Engine 3.

Side view of Foam 3 showing the handheld 1-1/2" High-Ex foam nozzle.

Foam 3 at the ready.

Engine 6 showing the hose bed fully loaded. Tanker 1 is just ahead on the outside apron.

Engine 6 in its glory.

Just "hamming it up" for a photo on Engine 6.

Another photo op with Tanker 1.

AN ARMY FIREFIGHTER IN VIETNAM 1970-1971

U. S. Army tank retriever pulling both the Napalm track and the Tank back to Station 1 after a burning mission.

Notice the red and white lettered sign on the Napalm track. It was another hot day for burning. The soldiers pulled off their fatigue shirts during the ride for a little relief.

Thirteen of the original soldier-firefighters with A/C Cha. I took the photo, and then ran out of film. And, I never got in a group photo later.

The original crew of Engine 3 with PAE A/C Cha on the left.

The leadership team. (L-R). A/C Cha, Chief Petersen, the author, and Tex.

Chief Petersen and A/C Cha with their recognition awards.

A/C Cha taking some photos of us.

Award time. Presenting A/C Cha with a recognition plaque.

AN ARMY FIREFIGHTER IN VIETNAM 1970-1971

Bunker gear donned, next to Foam 3 with Ricky the firehouse dog.

Our asbestos crash hoods. No reflective face shield. And, no gloves.

Engine 3's tailboard firemen wearing the duck canvas coats. I wore a Hypalon vinyl coat for ID purposes. Not enough standardized boots to go around. Notice the difference in footwear.

Long Binh Rescue 1.

Rear view of Rescue 1's interior.

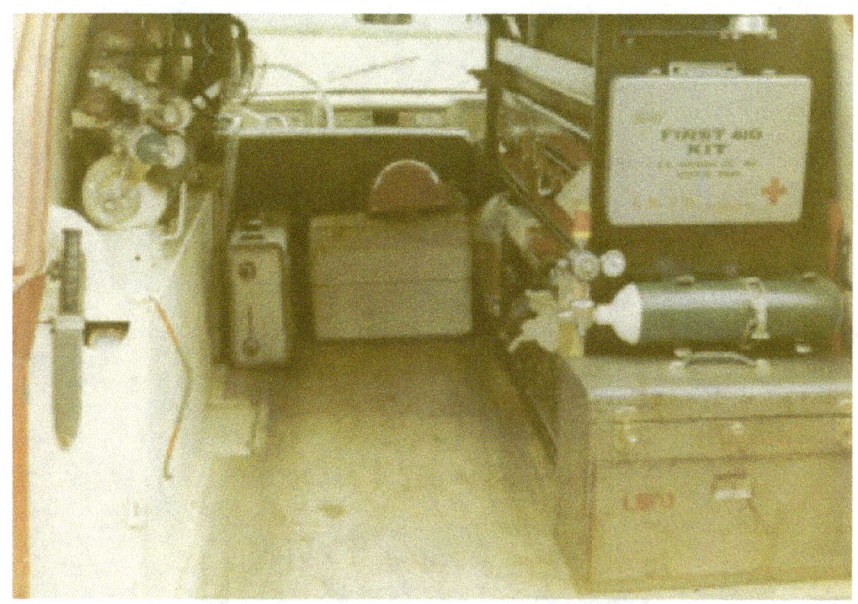

Close-up look of the inside of Rescue 1's equipment.

Ricky taking a nap by Engine 3.

Two of the Vietnamese PAE contract firemen covering Engine 6 with tarps.

Crash 1 at the ready at Station 2.

Crash 1. Notice the curved metal cover over the mid-ship mounted engine and pump assembly for ARFF "Pump'n'Roll" operations.

Posing at the Crash Station sign.

Rearview of Crash 1.

Business-end view of Jeep 2, showing the CB tank and hose reel, plus the 20 lb. Ansul extinguisher.

Rare view of Long Binh's airstrip from Station 2.

Rare view of the inner section of Long Binh's rotary wing section of aircraft.

A Huey coming in from a mission at Long Binh airfield.

AN ARMY FIREFIGHTER IN VIETNAM 1970-1971

A Cobra gunship at Long Binh airfield.

Hueys and Cobras at Long Binh airfield.

View of the rotary wing aircraft behind their protective barriers.

Chief Petersen starting to rebuild a reclaimed Fiberglas boat.

Chief Petersen (L) working on a section of the boat's Fiberglas, D/O Maull assisting him.

Ricky the firehouse dog. I was his buddy.

Christmas lights at Station 1 for 1970.

Christmas Eve truce lighting display.

Looking out from the apparatus floor near the Alarm Room doorway.
Engine 3 and Tanker 1 are outside. Note the foam can stacks.

Inside of Station 1 during Christmas 1970. Note the two doorways.
Center led to the bunkroom, and the Alarm Room was right of that.

Christmas decorations of 1970 above the apparatus bay stalls.

Christmas 1970 showing that Station 1's lone tree got a collection of lights.

AN ARMY FIREFIGHTER IN VIETNAM 1970-1971

Back of the stage for the 1970 Bob Hope Christmas show at Long Binh Amphitheater.

Bob Hope wearing a bright red ball cap going up the stairs to the stage.

General Westmoreland exiting his staff car for the Bob Hope show 1970 at Long Binh.

It was a crowd for sure! The tree and pole climbers did their thing.

Soldiers everywhere at the Long Binh Amphitheater 1970 Christmas show.

View of the back of the Amphitheatre stage entrance.
Notice the Christmas star above the stage.

One of the Din-a-Ling girls tasking a break. Dean Martin let Bob hope include them on his 1970 show. Great for soldier morale!

Of course, all of the Army photographers wanted a shot of the pretty Ding-a-Ling performer.

A Toyota Snorkel at Saigon Fire Brigade.

USA GMC Class A engines at Saigon Fire Brigade.
They were procured under the USAid program.

The modern Toyota Snorkel with a 1950 Mercedes-Benz-Metz German platform aerial ladder at Saigon Fire Brigade.

The hose repair shop at Saigon Fire Brigade.
A technician is repairing six inch LDH.

AN ARMY FIREFIGHTER IN VIETNAM 1970-1971

The Toyota Snorkel was extremely advanced for its time.
Notice the mid-ship mounted pump.

Looking down from the Watchtower of the Saigon Fire Brigade's compound.
Chief Petersen's pickup is on the left.

Jeep 6 of the Saigon Fire Brigade. The USAid program provided this type of smaller apparatus for navigating the narrow passageways of Saigon's old neighborhoods.

Saigon Fire Brigade's Watchtower.

The business end of one of the French built large capacity pumping engines.
Very powerful pumps for their time.

A Merryweather pumping engine from Great Britain.
Many free world countries sent apparatus to the Saigon Fire Brigade.

The inaugural in-country test between Protein and AFFF firefighting foams.

The Protein team on the left, with the AFF team on the right.

AN ARMY FIREFIGHTER IN VIETNAM 1970-1971

The AFFF team making good progress.

The Protein crew is struggling to make an initial foam blanket foothold.

Quite a difference in the fire foam performance.

Dr. Richard Tuve (white shirt) giving the AFFF crew some advice to not "plunge" the foam stream.

AN ARMY FIREFIGHTER IN VIETNAM 1970-1971

Not much firefighting progress for the Protein crew.

The test fires are out... Thanks to AFFF!

AFFF was finally used to suppress the Protein side of the test fire. Everyone was impressed.

Fire Station at Bien Hoa Air Force Base. It was a metal building, with A/C, and an asphalt apparatus apron.

Bien Hoa AFB foam trailer for foaming the runway. Rear view showing the pump and engine, with six downward facing foam application nozzles.

Air Force O-11A Crash truck at Bien Hoa Air Force Base.

Distant smoke from a pipeline fire, as seen from Station 1. The fire phone rang shortly after this photo was taken.

Climbing a "Church raise" on the 35' ladder for a drill.

AN ARMY FIREFIGHTER IN VIETNAM 1970-1971

At the top of the "Church raise".

We missed a lot of meals. My physique showed it.

Losing weight. I was down to 127 lbs., from a stateside 168 lbs.

I had a make-shift set of blues to wear when my fatigues did not come back in time from the laundry.

AN ARMY FIREFIGHTER IN VIETNAM 1970-1971

Another shot of my blues with my badge. Hurry up laundry!

Still have my waterproof matchstick holder. Check out the "Army green" matchstick heads!

The custom-made frontpiece from my MSA Crew Chief's helmet.

My treasured red helmet from Long Binh.

AN ARMY FIREFIGHTER IN VIETNAM 1970-1971

My treasured turnout coat from Long Binh. Olive drab duck canvas with leather trim and Scotchlite reflective striping.

Duty soft cap with a simple "Fire Dept" embroidered logo.

Model of the Tank with shell impact hole visible.

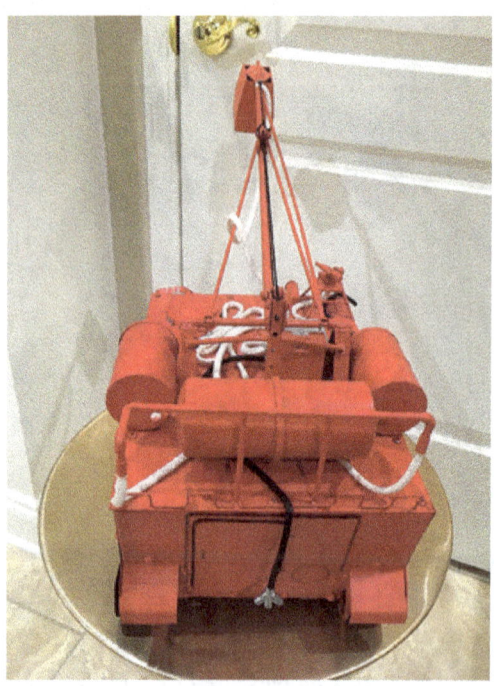

Rear view of the Fire Tank model showing foam tank, piping, and Water Thief.

AN ARMY FIREFIGHTER IN VIETNAM 1970-1971

Standing the Long Binh Fire Station's Pillbox on guard duty.

Checking the site of the .50 caliber machine gun on guard duty.

In fatigues, on watch, with fully automatic M-14 rifle and flak vest.

Going to take Engine 6 out for a road drive. Another hot sunny day.

ABOUT THE AUTHOR

Michael Louis Kuk, PhD, CFO, FIFireE, FABCHS, CHS-V, CNTA, CHSEMR is the retired fire chief for the Joint Readiness Training Center and US Army Garrison at Fort Polk, Louisiana. He has over fifty-five years of fire service experience, with fifty-plus years of chief officer tenure. In 1965 he became a Fire Explorer Scout and began his journey in the fire service. A United States Army Vietnam veteran, his professional service began at Fort Polk in 1969, going on to serve as the station chief for the US Army Firefighters' USARV Detachment at Long Binh, Vietnam during 1970 and 1971. After his military obligation was completed, he served in his hometown department of Clinton, Iowa, as a Tillerman and one of the first EMTs. In Louisiana, he served as the fire chief for OLIN Chemicals and PPG Industries in Lake Charles, and the first chief of the Ward 1 Fire Protection District of Moss Bluff. He was the first chief in Louisiana to have active duty career and volunteer women firefighters, including officers and EMT's. His work history also includes serving as the last fire chief at Savanna Army Depot, Illinois, and the prison chief at Fort Leavenworth, Kansas. In 1998 he was selected as Army Firefighter of the Year. In 2009 he was the first inductee into the US Army Fire Chiefs Hall of

Fame. The Military Firefighter Heritage Foundation inducted him into the Military Firefighter Hall of Fame in 2018. Chief Kuk is the founding member and chair of the Federal Firefighters Memorial Committee (established 1994) and the Federal Fire Chaplain. During the combined Department of Defense Fire and Emergency Services annual conferences with the International Association of Fire Chiefs, he served as a primary committeeman for the Pentagon and was the event's Master Musician. Within the Fort Polk Directorate of Emergency Services, he served as the DES Chaplain, and as the chair of the CBRNE Working Group. He presently serves as the Senior Fire Chaplain for the Vernon Parish Fire Protection District and was the district's founding Chief Fire Chaplain and Director of the Firefighter Honor Guard. He is a charter board member of the Louisiana Fire Chaplains Network, the Adjutant Command Chaplain, Regional Director, and the Flying Squad Commander. In addition, he continues to serve as the musical director and protocol advisor for the Louisiana State Fire Marshal's Walk of Honor Foundation, which oversees the annual memorial service and memorial site in Baton Rouge (established 2004). He also serves on the State Fire Marshal's Steering Committee and has been asked to serve as the first curator for the proposed State Fire Marshal Firefighter Museum. In December 2012, he received the State Fire Marshal's Fire Chief of the Year award. Chief Kuk holds the honored title of Fellow for the American Board for Certification in Homeland Security. He is also a fellow in the esteemed Institution of Fire Engineers of Great Britain, being the only chief fire officer to hold dual fellowships in the United States. The Commission on Professional Credentialing awarded the designation of Chief Fire Officer to him in 2004 and continues to be re-designated ever since his initial acceptance. Chief Kuk has been a published fire service author since 1974, with over a hundred peer-reviewed articles, including booklets and manuals. He has conducted extensive research on firefighting history since Roman times. His landmark article about the true story of Saint Florian, the Firefighter's Patron, appeared in the May 2000 issue of *Firehouse* magazine. As a result of his extensive travels and research regarding the Holy Florian and his Roman firefighters, Chief Kuk is recognized as the world authority on Roman firefighters. He also writes about Federal and Department of Defense firefighting subjects, including Homeland Security. Overall, his writings have touched historical, technical, and inspirational subjects. His writings have been published in countless fire publications, including many newspapers and other non-fire service magazines and periodicals. He served as a contributing editor for *Fire Service Digest* for many years and is a contributing author for *Fire Engineering, Firehouse, Vintage Fire Truck & Equipment* magazines, and the *Joker Stand Journal*. A 2006 Inductee of the '50 and '60s Rock 'n' Roll Hall of Fame with his band of the 1960s, the Union Jacks, he continues to perform as a master musician at firefighter, military, and civil ceremonies and events. He performed all of the inaugural music for the Illinois Firefighter Memorial Dedication Ceremony on May 13, 1999, at Springfield, Illinois, and pleasantly surprised all attendees with a special rendition of *Backdraft* as the opening theme. He performed this motion picture movie score by ear and memory on his synthesizers, since no printed music was available at that time. Every June he returns to his home state of Iowa to perform music for the Iowa Firefighters Association's Annual Memorial Service and has been serving in that role since the first ceremony of June 1995. He also serves as their protocol/ ceremony and music adviser and writes historical and inspirational inserts for their annual memorial brochure. In June 2012, he received the IFA's Outstanding Fire Service Individual Award for his steadfast and long-term commitment. In 2021 the Marquis Who's Who awarded him the Top Professional recognition in the Top Military Awards program. And also in 2021, the Marquis Who's Who Publication Board bestowed the Albert Nelson Marquis Lifetime Achievement Award to Kuk, because of his lifelong commitment to the International Fire Service. A lifetime member of the International Association of

Fire Chiefs since 1977, Kuk has led volunteer, combination, industrial, military, and federal fire departments. His musical talents were a major part of the IAFC's conference for seventeen years. He is recognized as our nation's top-performing firefighter-musician, whereas he continues to perform at countless ceremonies honoring firefighters everywhere. And his hobby is collecting fire memorabilia, especially items pertaining to Saint Florian, and corresponding with over fifty fire service pen pals internationally. His custom-built home, with a full fire sprinkler system, is a true personal fire museum, and a separate detached building houses the rest of the collection. Both structures are full of treasures gathered throughout his journey in the international fire service. He hosts many traveling fire service personnel during any given time, who enjoy experiencing a firsthand look at this memorabilia. An extensive library fills the twenty-foot high "hose tower" portion of the home, and it includes a library ladder! His quest for international fire service education and historical note found him serving as the Director of Brigade International, thereby leading delegations to countries such as South Africa, Germany, and Austria during the '90s. He recently served as a delegate for FireNet when that group visited Poland in 2016. A long-time member of the Fire Buffs of Illinois, a founding member of the Fire Museum of Greater Chicago, and a member of SPAAMFAA, he attends numerous musters and related activities as his time and travel limitations permit. His unique chaplaincy was part of the twilight ceremony when the Wildland Firefighters Memorial site was dedicated in May 2000 at the Interagency Fire Center in Boise, Idaho. He used special holy water from the ground spring of the Saint Florian grotto in Linz, Austria, to bless the three wildland firefighter statues and overall grounds. Of special note, he worked Ground Zero in November 2001, supporting the overall chaplaincy efforts there with the ranking FDNY chaplain. He is a disabled Vietnam veteran as a result of his active duty time in the US Army as a Combat Firefighter in that theater of war.

AN ARMY FIREFIGHTER IN VIETNAM 1970-1971

www.ingramcontent.com/pod-product-compliance
Lightning Source LLC
LaVergne TN
LVHW020417070526
838199LV00055B/3649